The World's Great
River Journeys

The World's Great
River Journeys

50 scenic voyages along the waterways of 6 continents

Nick Dalton and Deborah Stone

JOHN BEAUFOY PUBLISHING

CONTENTS

Introduction   6

Europe   **8**
Amsterdam's waterways   10
The Caledonian Canal   14
The Danube: *Nuremberg to Budapest*   16
The Danube: *Budapest to Bucharest*   22
The Dnieper   28
The Douro   30
The Elbe   36
The Gironde and The Dordogne   40
The Gironde and The Garonne   42
The Guadalquivir   44
The Main   48
The Marne   52
The Moselle   54
The Po   58
The Rhine: *Amsterdam to Mainz*   60
The Rhine: *Mainz to Basel*   66
The Rhône and The Saône   72
The Sava   78
The Seine   80
The Shannon   86
The Thames   88
The Tisza   92
The Volga and The Svir   94

North America   **100**
The Columbia   102
The Hudson   106
The Illinois   110
The Mississippi: *New Orleans to Memphis*   114
The Mississippi: *Memphis to St Louis*   120
The St Johns   124
The St Lawrence   126
The Yukon   130

South America   **134**
The Amazon   136
The Orinoco   142

Africa   **146**

The Chobe   148
The Congo   150
The Niger   152
The Nile   154
The Senegal   160
The Zambezi   162

Asia   **166**

The Ayeyarwady   168
The Brahmaputra   172
The Chindwin   174
The Ganges   176
The Kinabatangan   180
The Upper Mekong: *Laos to China*   182
The Lower Mekong: *Vietnam to Cambodia*   184
The Red River   188
The Yangtze   190

Australia & New Zealand   **196**

The Murray   198
The Whanganui   202

Who Goes Where   204
Index   205

Introduction

Have you ever wondered where a river really goes? We all know rivers, at least where they touch our lives whether in reality or on film – the romantic Seine in Paris; the big, boisterous Thames as it cuts through London; the mighty Mississippi rolling through the USA. We've all seen them in some form or other. Yet where do they go when they're out of sight? And where do they come from?

Almost all the world's major rivers cross hundreds of miles – some of them thousands – as they pass through mountain ranges, negotiate deserts, irrigate farmland and bring cheer to historic towns and cities that have sprung up along their path. Some are beholden to one nation; others flow through a string of countries as they make their way across continents.

River cruising as a way to explore is far from new, yet it's taken off like never before with fleets of new ships criss-crossing countries. It may be boom time but it will never disturb the peace and quiet, as even the biggest ships only carry around 200 people, so this is a discreet travel boom in what amount to floating boutique hotels.

The result is the ability to truly see a river to the full, such as the Rhine, all the way from Amsterdam by the North Sea to Basel in Switzerland; going with the flow on the Danube, taking in 10 countries from Germany to Ukraine and the Black Sea; travelling on the Mekong through Vietnam and Cambodia and Laos and into China; or marvelling at the wildlife reserves in Africa or the impressive ancient history of Egypt. Taking a river voyage is like a grand road trip without the wheels, watching the countryside slip past at a much gentler pace. Castles and gorges, glittering night-time cities and sun-drenched beaches – there's little that can't be seen as you slip through the heart of nations (capital cities such as Vienna and Bratislava and Belgrade) with daily opportunities to explore.

And yet for every river that is host to cutting-edge vessels and mainstream voyages, there's another that stays out of the limelight. It might be the Yukon, making its way through Canada and Alaska (even the stretches that can easily be navigated are generally so far off the beaten track as to keep most tourists away). Or Africa's rivers such as the Senegal or the Niger, where most river traffic is restricted to small boats with the occasional steamer or ferry service having a colonial air. Or the old-time adventurer feel of Australia and New Zealand. Even some of Europe's rivers are lost in time – not least the meandering route of the rivers, waterways and lakes that snake across Russia.

But wherever you are, there's a river to be run. Whether you're passing through the Sahara sands in Mali as the Niger approaches Timbuktu, gazing up at the skyscrapers of Manhattan at the end of a Hudson voyage or finding yourself lost in the sea-like expanse of the Amazon, there's always something different to marvel at. Here's the chance to find out where that river has come from, where it's going to – and how to experience it yourself.

Nick Dalton and Deborah Stone

China's Yangtze runs through the towering scenery of the spectacular Three Gorges

An *Emerald Star* cruise heads into Budapest past the ornate Hungarian Parliament

Europe

AMSTERDAM'S WATERWAYS

Lose yourself in the maze between the city of canals and Antwerp

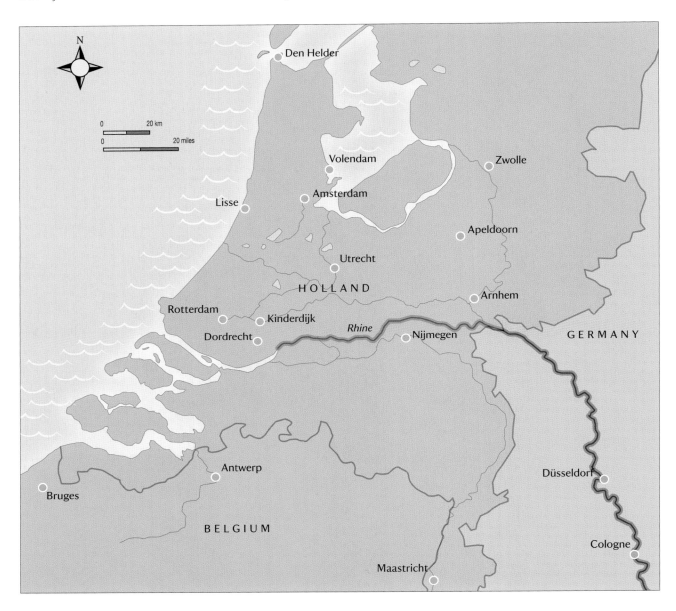

As a city with almost as many canals to its name as streets, Amsterdam is purpose-built for river cruises. Ships leave from the Port of Amsterdam, within easy walking distance of some of the city's most important tourist sights, then sail down the Rhine Canal to dip into the River Rhine and follow the maze of Dutch canals, rivers and inland seas.

Virtually every cruise line has a Dutch Waterways itinerary and also offers cruises from Amsterdam that cross from the Netherlands into Belgium. These head for Antwerp on the River Scheldt where the central square – Grote Markt – is lined with Guild Houses and has a 16th-century town hall. From here ships may also sail along the River Scheldt to Ghent, with its glorious medieval squares, and some will offer excursions to the Renaissance city of Bruges.

With a waterways cruise it can be difficult to pinpoint exactly where you are, whether you're on a river or a canal, and where you're heading, but the pancake-flat scenery, the ancient windmills and the slow pace of life make this a fascinating region in which to cruise.

The tall, narrow buildings that line Amsterdam's canal banks date back to the Netherlands' Golden Age in the 17th century, when the city was expanding so fast it had to build up rather than out. Trade with the Baltic states and Amsterdam's East India and West India Companies made the Netherlands Europe's richest colonial power for almost all of the 1600s. Canal houses were used as warehouses or shops as well as homes. The wealthy merchants' most

Below: Bruges' Groenerei canal with the medieval Belfry, a former treasury and lookout tower with 366 steps

lasting legacy, apart from those iconic buildings, is the hundreds of old masters' paintings they commissioned that now fill galleries such as the incomparable Rijksmuseum, where Rembrandt's *The Night Watch* takes centre stage. The Rembrandt House Museum gives a glimpse of life during this extraordinary period, when Dutch ships controlled the lucrative spice trade in the East and merchants had so much money that a craze for rare tulips led to one of the most famous investment bubbles the world has ever seen. Tulip bulbs from Turkey changed

hands for more money than houses, making fortunes for some traders, until 'Tulip Mania' crashed in February 1637.

During the Golden Age a wind-powered industrial revolution enabled the Netherlands to pump water out of its below-sea-level land to boost agriculture and these windmills can still be seen along the river banks – nowhere better than at Kinderdijk on the River Noord, where the UNESCO World Heritage Site has 19 historic windmills. Dutch agriculture flourished thanks to cleverly engineered dykes and dams, which has led to one of its biggest exports: flowering bulbs and cut flowers. In some areas the bulb fields are all the colours of the rainbow as flowers are left uncut so that the more valuable bulbs will grow fatter.

Another delightful collection of windmills, along with historic wooden houses and barns to give the feel of a village, is Zaanse Schans, just to the north of Amsterdam.

From March until May millions visit the Keukenhof Gardens near Lisse, on the other side of the city, which are planted with seven million bulbs annually to create rivers of hyacinths, swathes of daffodils and narcissi as well as, of course, tulips. Excursions to Keukenhof from Rotterdam on the River Rhine are popular when the spring gardens are open but, for the non-horticulturalists, Rotterdam has lots on offer.

Although almost completely destroyed by air raids during the Second World War, the Netherlands' second largest city is now best known for its outrageous modern architecture, such as the Cube Houses by architect Piet Blom. But there are also pockets of history, such as the open-air Harbour Museum where former Holland America Line ship SS *Rotterdam* is now a hotel and restaurant.

Other typical Dutch Waterways river stops include Arnhem, scene of the Second World War's Operation Market Garden in 1944. The Allies attempted to gain control over several river bridges to free Dutch towns and break through German lines but despite some success, the

crossing at Arnhem proved a bridge too far – to quote the title of the 1977 war film starring Sean Connery.

Airborne Museum Hartenstein near Arnhem is a must for those fascinated by the war, while another popular excursion is to the Palace of Het Loo near Apeldoorn, home of William III of Orange. William was the Dutch royal who became joint ruler of England with his English wife Mary II in 1688 after deposing James II, Mary's pro-Catholic father.

Cruises may stop at Volendam, a jaunty little fishing village on the shores of the Ijsselmeer – the inland sea that use to be called Zuiderzee. There's a seaside atmosphere to the waterfront, which is full of bars, restaurants and souvenir shops. Nearby is Edam, where a small factory museum tells the story of Holland's most famous cheese.

The Golden Age shaped many other Dutch river towns, such as Dordrecht, the Netherlands' oldest town, which has more than 1,000 historic buildings. The warehouses and merchant buildings around the historic quays here have been transformed into cafés, restaurants and artisan shops in a typically neat and flower-filled Dutch style.

Crossing the Dutch border into Belgium, a lovely day out can be made of a visit to Antwerp, with its old quarter featuring a medieval maze of narrow streets. As well as the historic Grote Markt, there's the Diamond Museum, explaining how Antwerp became the focus of Europe's diamond trade, and the home of 17th-century painter Sir Peter Paul Rubens.

Below: The colourful windmills of Zaanse Schans, a recreated village including houses, artisan workshops and a museum

THE CALEDONIAN CANAL

The Highlands, loch, stock and barrel

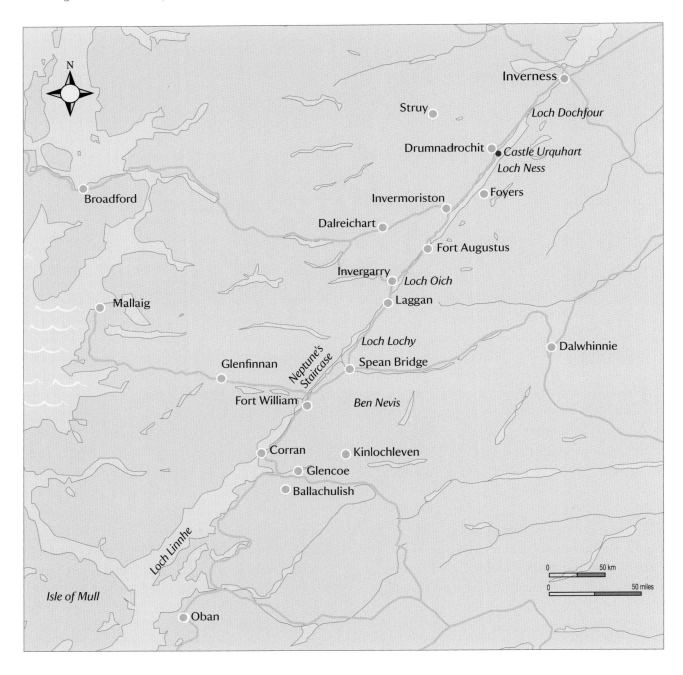

Right: The hotel barge *Spirit of Scotland* negotiates a narrow stretch of Loch Oich against a misty mountain backdrop

This man-made waterway simply connects a series of bodies of water – Scotland's fabled lochs – to provide a coast-to-coast traverse that unites the most spectacular scenery with awesome Victorian engineering.

The Caledonian, a protected ancient monument, was masterminded in the early 19th century by engineer Thomas Telford, runs 60 miles (90km) from Loch Linnhe on the west coast to Inverness on the east, cutting through the Grampian Mountains. Two-thirds of its length is natural, through Loch Ness, Loch Dochfour, Loch Oich and Loch Lochy. It passes by Ben Nevis, Britain's loftiest mountain at 4,411ft (1,345km), and through Neptune's Staircase, an extraordinary set of eight locks. From end to end there are 36 locks, four aqueducts and 10 bridges.

The canal is navigable by small ships, allowing week-long cruises aboard vessels such as the mahogany-rich luxury of *Lord of the Glens* and European Waterways' hotel barge *Spirit of Scotland*. It is also popular with self-hire cruisers.

Oban (the starting point for some cruises) sits on the west coast. Ships head past islands as the grand waters narrow, first passing the peak of Glencoe, then Ben Nevis to the south, arriving in the canal at the town of Fort William. The surroundings are impressive; the greens and purples of the mountains mingle with the often brooding sky. They can be enjoyed at leisure at Neptune's Staircase, a 90-minute passage during which vessels rise 64ft (20m).

The journey passes through villages in gentle surroundings as well as the wildest of highland scenery – Loch Lochy is nine miles (15km) long and half a mile (0.8km) wide. And Loch Ness, awash with mysterious grandeur and, as legend tells, the Loch Ness Monster, is three times as wide and 23 miles (37km) long. One of the world's leading beauty spots, it is reached after descending a flight of locks in the pretty town of Fort Augustus. The remains of Castle Urquhart, dating back to the 15th century, sit on a headland and offer splendid views.

Having your own boat allows time to explore to the full, docking at spots away from the busy tourist centres, while cruises offer a number of excursions. At Corpach it's possible to take a ride on the West Highland Railway over the 21-arch Glenfinnan Viaduct.

This is one of the truly inspiring inland journeys, deserving of a dram of single malt, whether you're on deck in the golden-age, cruise-ship surroundings of *Lord of the Glens* or sitting at the Lock Inn by the locks of Fort Augustus watching the action.

THE DANUBE
NUREMBERG TO BUDAPEST

A journey through wine country and the towns and cities of the Austro-Hungarian Monarchy

The Danube is the classic European river, heading through beautiful countryside and stylish cities, and offering easily accessible mainstream cruises. The river starts in Germany's Black Forest, where the rivers Brigach and Breg meet. It's then a journey of 1,700 miles (2,800km) to the Black Sea via the Danube Delta in Romania and Ukraine. The most popular itinerary runs between Nuremberg in Germany and Budapest in Hungary, taking in the capital cities of Austria and Slovakia – Vienna and Bratislava – plus other delightful towns. Longer cruises may go all the way down to near the Black Sea or at least to a river port within striking distance of Romania's capital Bucharest (see p. 20).

Some cruises begin at Bamberg, the town at the start of the Main-Danube canal, but this is more often included in a River Main and River Rhine trip. The UNESCO-listed medieval streets here are enchanting and the canal, cutting through fairly rugged, forested, countryside to Nuremberg, is quietly pleasing.

Nuremberg's medieval centre and 11th-century fort were rebuilt virtually brick by brick after the Second World War, as well as the huge Gothic cathedral near the Market Square. The medieval atmosphere within the walled area is exactly what you would expect of a town with a tradition of toy-making that reaches back several centuries. There's a superb Toy Museum, where you can follow the development from carved wooden toys to the more sophisticated tin toys of the industrialised age and more recent plastic incarnations.

It's no surprise that in December the Christmas market in Nuremberg is one of the biggest and best in Germany. But Nuremberg has another fascination, and much of that centres on the Nazi Party Rally Grounds and the eerie feeling you can get standing on the spot where Hitler held his supporters spellbound. Nearby is the massive Congress Hall, inspired by Rome's Coliseum, and which should have had a self-supporting roof and seats for 50,000 but was

never finished. Now one wing has a permanent exhibition of films and photographs of Nazi rallies, many of them once held just feet away.

The Main-Danube Canal passes through the eastern edge of town and it is still 70 miles (110km) until you reach the Danube, at the little town of Kelheim. First call after this is Regensburg, where the river splits into several channels as it passes through; the arched Roman stone bridge connecting the island old town. This is very much a Roman town – as you can see in the various archaeological digs – and the oldest town on the Danube, which sustained remarkably little damage in the Second World War. There are the remains of the Roman wall and a Romanesque town gate, Porta Praetoria, along with the UNESCO-listed centre's 13th-century town hall, where German emperors held court, and several Patrician tower-like houses – owned by aristocratic Italian merchants – from the 12th to the 14th century. Stop for

Top: Regensburg, Germany, one of Europe's best preserved medieval cities with twin-spired cathedral and Stone Bridge

Above: Many Danube cruises start at Passau, a pretty town dominated by 13th-century hill fortress Veste Oberhaus

Regensburger sausages at the historic Sausage Kitchen next to the stone bridge.

As it heads for Austria, the Danube runs through dramatic, steep, rocky cliffs studded with tall pine trees, although there are also green hills stretching off into the distance cloaked in trees. In places the riverbanks are flat, with rustic-looking holiday homes. Every now and again a large fortified building looms into view, testament to the constant fighting between rival princedoms long ago. Equally as significant as the fortified homes are the impressive churches and cathedrals that are the focus of many of the river towns.

Passau, in Germany but on the Austrian border, is dominated by St Stephen's Cathedral, which is unusual in having two distinct architectural styles: the back is Gothic, the front a more modern Baroque style. The mix stems from a fire in 1662, which burnt down half the town as well as half the cathedral. Inside it is spectacularly ornate, with huge statues at the top of the columns and painted ceilings with lots of plump cherubs, and imagery that appears indecipherable to the untrained eye. It also has the world's biggest church organ, with 17,300 pipes. Passau has the River Danube on one side and the River Inn arriving on the other, coming from Innsbruck, creating a particularly pretty

Top: Schoenbuehel Castle, near Melk, is one of the many ancient sights on this stretch of the river

Right: *Emerald Sky* passes vine-covered slopes dotted with castles along the Wachau Valley

Opposite: Benedictine Melk Abbey sits on a rocky outcrop above the river

Right: Vienna State Opera is just one of the many sights to see on a tour of what is one of the truly great river cities

setting and with the early 13th-century Veste Oberhaus fortress looking down from its hilltop perch.

Next is Linz, with its ornate Baroque old town. This is Austria's third largest city that is fairly industrial but does has the superb Ars Electronica Centre – a museum of technology with robotics, space exploration and interactive design at its core. Also by the river is the ultra-modern Lentos Art Museum with paintings by 19th-century Austrians such as Gustav Klimt as well as work from the Austrian Expressionist movement of the 1920s and 1930s.

Melk couldn't be more different: a tiny town with a huge 11th-century Benedictine Abbey sitting on a hill, a place that is a treasure-house of medieval manuscripts, gold and silver church artefacts and a Baroque church that is completely over the top.

Dürnstein is another small river town but with a big reputation. Surrounded by vineyards, the picturesque town is in the middle of the Wachau Valley – an area thought to be so beautiful that it has been UNESCO listed. In Dürnstein enjoy the quaint shops and cafés but also climb the hill behind the town to the ruined castle where Richard the Lionheart was held on his way back from the Crusades and only released when a 100,000-mark ransom was paid.

The Wachau Valley stretches from Melk to the town of Krems. Its castles, monasteries and small towns are all protected by the UNESCO listing. Krems, an ancient wine town, has the obligatory abbey, beautiful churches, pretty squares and museums but it fades into insignificance compared to the architectural treasures of Vienna.

It would take a week to see all that Vienna has to offer. This imperial city – centre of the Hapsburg Empire and adopted home of musicians such as Mozart, Beethoven and Strauss – is full of history, music and art. The Hofburg is a vast complex of museums including the Imperial Apartments, Hofburg Treasury and Imperial Chapel as well as the Spanish Riding School within its grounds.

St Stephen's Cathedral is the main landmark and a symbol of no-nonsense Gothic stability compared to the Baroque confection of Karlskirche. There's the grandiose Vienna State Opera while the National Theatre has a staircase decorated with frescoes by Gustav and Ernst Klimt. There's more Klimt in the Belvedere Museum – two

Baroque palaces full of art (where his famous painting, *The Kiss*, hangs), while on the edge of town the Schönbrunn Palace has 1,441 rooms and park-like gardens. Vienna's town hall is also a fabulous neo-Gothic building, where the city's largest Christmas market is held every December, its windows transformed into a giant advent calendar and the park outside strung with lights and decorations.

Next is Slovakia's capital, Bratislava, which has an old town like a scene from a Hans Christian Andersen fairy tale. You can climb up to the hilltop castle or visit its medieval cathedral and walk along the remnants of the old city wall. The one remaining gateway to what was a walled city looks like a white tower topped by an extravagant spire and the large central square houses the 14th-century City Hall, now a museum. There are more museums in the castle which also has views over the old city's red roofs and the Soviet high-rise flats on the other side of the river.

Just south of the city, on a peninsula near where Slovakia, Austria and Hungary meet, sits Danubiana Meulensteen Art Museum. In the shape of a Roman galley, it is packed with modern art and has gardens with fabulous views.

And then there is Budapest, a place of sheer charm and elegance. There's a real thrill to sailing past the neo-Gothic spires of Hungary's Parliament, one of the most iconic sights on Europe's rivers. It's beautiful by day and magical by night, when it is lit up like a particularly tasteful Christmas tree – as are the historic bridges that cross the Danube, such as the distinctive Chain Bridge that connects the old towns of Buda and Pest.

Below: Danubiana Meulensteen Art Museum sits on a peninsula just to the south of Bratislava

THE DANUBE

BUDAPEST TO BUCHAREST

Great cities and the heritage of Eastern Europe

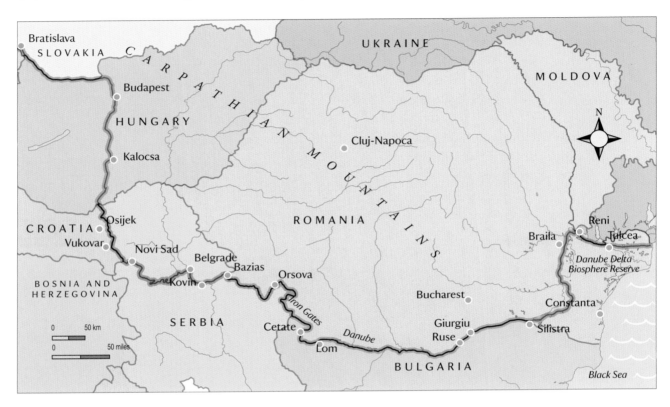

The Danube sweeps through the city of Budapest, a great curve between hilltop Buda and more modern Pest. Some river cruise ships dock on the Buda side, opposite Parliament (handy for walks up the hill into the old town); others in Pest, between the Elisabeth and Liberty bridges, just round the corner from the big market hall, where you can buy strings of dried chillis, bottles of plum brandy and other treats.

A day spent in Budapest is a day to remember. On the must-do list is the museum quarter near the Castle Palace on the Buda side of the river, where the fortification-like Fisherman's Bastion is the perfect viewing platform to look out over to Pest, on the other side of the river, where you'll find stylish shopping streets such as Váci utca and Budapest's café society.

Gelert Hill, also on the Buda side, has fabulous views down to the river and you can see the Pest side laid out as far as Heroes' Square with its statues of Magyar chieftains and other important Hungarians, which is the entrance to City Park and several museums within it. Catch a bus to Memento Park, an open-air museum of statues from Hungary's Communist era. It's an astonishing place. There are several thermal baths in Budapest but the Art Nouveau Gellert Baths or Belle Epoque Szechenyi Spa Baths are the ones to go for.

From Budapest the Danube flows south through Hungary into Serbia where it is the border with Croatia and becomes the border between Bulgaria and Romania until it drains into the Black Sea not far from Romania's border with Ukraine.

Above: Remains of the riverside fort in Osijek, Croatia, on the Drava near its confluence with the Danube

Most river cruise ships only go as far as Giurgiu in Romania, though, before transferring you by coach to Romania's capital, Bucharest, where the deposed Communist Party leader Nicolae Ceaucescu's Parliament Palace – with an extraordinary 3,000 rooms – can be seen, along with Revolution Square where the 1989 riots that ended Romania's Communist regime took place.

Day trips on the Danube delta are available and some cruise lines also venture down there before returning to Budapest.

South of Budapest and six miles (10km) from the Danube is Kalocsa, surrounded by fields growing paprika – the bell pepper essential for Hungary's national dish of goulash. There's even a paprika museum – and plenty of shops selling paprika souvenirs.

On the Croatian side there's Vukovar, the country's biggest river port, where the sights are rather more serious. The town is a living memorial to the 1991 battle of Vukovar during Croatia's war of independence in the early 1990s. Some of the shelled and bullet-riddled buildings, including a water tower, have been left in ruins as a reminder of the brutality of the break-up of Yugoslavia.

From Vukovar there are often excursions to Osijek, on the River Drava, 12 miles (20km) away. The countryside changes from marshlands around the Danube, where Nature Park Kopacki is home to many species of bird, to vineyards and forests with Osijek retaining a flavour of the

Austro-Hungarian Empire. The town has Vienna-influenced Baroque architecture, although much was damaged during the 1990s war.

Farther downriver on the Serbian side is Novi Sad, where the Petrovaradin Citadel towers over the water. There's a path up for great views. Puzzle at the unusual tower clock face (the long hand is for hours and the short one for minutes so that fishermen could see the time) and visit the underground tunnels. Novi Sad has an Austro-Hungarian feel, too, with the Gallery of Matica Srpska displaying Serbian art from the 18th to 20th centuries and Trg Slobode – Freedom Square – home to the neo-Renaissance City Hall and neo-Gothic Church of the Name of Mary.

There are pedestrianised streets with lovely shops, cafés and bars, and a beach. Nearby are several small wineries, where you can buy wine and honey, and many monasteries. Some, such as Krusedol, are open for tours.

It will take a little longer to see the sights of Belgrade, Serbia's capital. Overlooking the river is the Kalemegdan fortress, a symbol of Belgrade's strategic importance from Roman times onward. The fortress is on a hill where the River Sava meets the Danube, which is where the Roman city of Singidunum was founded. Much of this site is now a park containing museums and galleries, restaurants and Belgrade Zoo. From the fortress you can stroll down Knez Mihailova Street – Prince Michael Street – past shops, cafés and restaurants plus handsome old palaces, right into the centre of town.

Among the most fascinating places to visit is the Museum of Yugoslavia, which explains how Yugoslavia was created from several Balkan states after the Second World War. Photographs, art and other treasures are used to illustrate the often uneasy Communist alliance. Marshal Tito's Mausoleum, the Yugoslav President's tomb, is in the grounds of the museum. Also worth seeing is the Serbian Orthodox Church of St Sava, one of the largest Orthodox

Left: Sleek, modern cruise ship *Scenic Opal* enters the age-old Iron Gate, dividing Romania and Serbia, a truly dramatic sight

churches in the world and the Museum of Contemporary Art. But Belgrade's independent shops and cafés are also lovely to explore, particularly because of the city's fascination for coffee – possibly thanks to its Turkish occupation in the 16th and 17th centuries.

Not far downriver is another of the Danube's most famous sights: Djerdap Gorge, better-known as Iron Gate, a scenic stretch between Romania and Serbia set in the Djerdap National Park, which runs along the Danube from Golubacki Grad to the dam at Sip. The gorge is in fact three gorges separated by ravines that continue for nearly 65 miles (100km), set against the dramatic backdrop of the Carpathian Mountains. The river at Iron Gate – at the third gorge, Kazan – is less than 500ft (150m) wide with cliffs towering almost 500ft (300m) above it.

While the countryside is picturesque, there are parts of the Danube here that are very industrialised, particularly the Djerdap hydroelectric power station and the huge locks that have made the river much safer for navigation.

Once through the locks, though, you are marvelling at the narrowness of Iron Gorge and, farther downriver, at the massive rock sculpture of Decebalus, last king of Dacia (modern-day Romania), who fought the Roman Empire to maintain his country's independence. The carving is at Bor, Romania, on a cliff overlooking the river and is a popular stop-off during river trips.

The old port of Cetate in Romania is also fascinating. Port buildings, left derelict during the Communist era, have been transformed into Cetate Cultural Port. Starting with poetry workshops in the late 1990s, it is now the site of cultural events such as the SoNoRo classical music festival, the Divan Film Festival, creative writing camps and live music.

The Danube now heads for Rousse (or Ruse) in Bulgaria, on the opposite side of the river to Romania's Giurgiu. Rousse's neo-Baroque and neo-Rococo architecture is to thank for the city's nickname of Little Vienna, although one of its most interesting attractions is the National

Transport Museum housed in Bulgaria's first railway station. Exhibits include the carriages of Tsar Boris III and Tsar Ferdinand, and the Turkish sultan Abdul Aziz, as well as old locomotives.

Meanwhile, over the river in Giurgiu there is little to do except take a trip to Romania's capital, Bucharest, about 37 miles (60km) away. The massive Palace of Parliament is a must-see and there are guided tours to marvel at the marble-built rooms and gold-encrusted décor. You can see how the people of Bucharest lived before the 1989 Revolution in places like the Peasant Museum, Roma Culture Museum and Bucharest Communism Museum.

But just as pre-Second World War Bucharest was known as the Paris of the East due to its Art Nouveau architecture – much of that now gone – today it is gaining a reputation as the new Berlin, thanks to its nightlife and attractions. Much of this is focused on the old town, where there are still some elegant pre-Communist buildings. But as tourism in Romania continues to grow, look out for places like the Future Museum – where artists and curators display unexplored concepts and unknown phenomena.

Some cruises head another 90 miles (145km) to Silistra, where the Danube splits in two at the start of the Danube Delta. The scenery is flat as the twin channels head northeast, at one point briefly rejoining before creating a big rural island just outside the town of Braila, where (the river reunited once more) a little car ferry chugs across.

The river then enters Ukraine and forms the border with Romania for the last few miles of land before the Danube Delta Biosphere Reserve, a vast area of marshes and lakes, home to wild cats, wild boar and otters as well as a huge array of birdlife including pelicans and swans. The temperatures are warm and the Danube has disappeared into the Black Sea.

Below: Bucharest's colossal Communist-era Palace of Parliament, which also contains three museums

THE DNIEPER
From Russia to the Black Sea

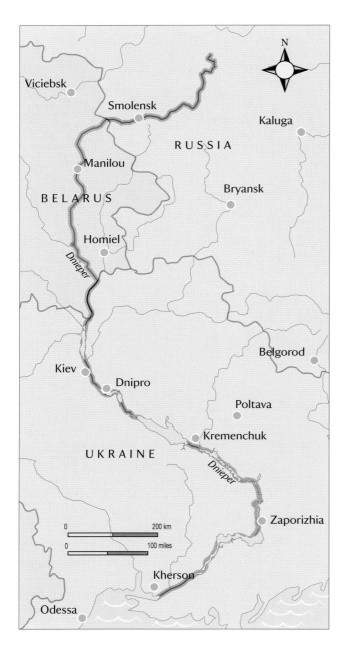

The Dnieper is one of Europe's major yet lesser-known waterways, emerging near the Russian city of Smolensk then running more than 1,300 miles (2,200km) across Russia, Belarus and Ukraine to the Black Sea. The river (the third longest in Europe after the Danube and the Volga) is a major transport link and all but the final 100 miles (160km) nearest the source are navigable with major ships able to reach the inland port of Kiev, Ukraine's capital.

This is a gorgeous city with plenty of exceptional architecture, much of it religious, such as the Italianate grandeur and golden trimmings of St Andrew's Church, more a cathedral, sitting on a hilltop.

To both the south and the north of Kiev the river opens out several times to lake-like proportions up to 12 miles (20km) wide and just to the south there are dozens of islands. The city itself is made up of many islands divided by a multitude of channels and dotted with jetties, man-made beaches and parks. On the western side, the older part of the city, the streets give way to the tree-covered Kiev Hills, cut with ravines and small rivers.

Cruises are increasingly popular on the lower stretch, entirely within Ukraine, though some major companies

Left: Grandiose St Andrew's Church sits on a hilltop and gazes out across the city of Kiev with splendid views of the river

Below: Zaporozhian Cossack Museum, on protected Khortytsia Island is a place to see horsemanship demonstrations

offer voyages all the way from Kiev to the Black Sea. The journey is a magical one that switches at the drop of a Cossack hat from wide and open expanses to narrow stretches curling around hills and between rocky walls. Onion-domed churches poke their heads up with regularity and there are big cities thanks to this being an ancient trade route from Moscow to the sea (and part of an even longer one, from Scandinavia to Constantinople).

First up is Kremenchuk, 175 miles (280km) from Kiev, an industrial city yet looking across at the green islands of Landschaftnyy Park and even with a beach. Dnipro is also an industrial hub, whose streets have a muscular style, full of 50s, Stalinist-era architecture, but given a new charm by the more contemporary buildings. The city of Zaporizhia sits on another narrow stretch. Near the town, Kichkas Bridge spans the narrowest part at 'Wolf Throat' with its rapids and locks, just before eight-mile (12km) Khortytsia Island, a National Reserve, whose lush setting is the ceremonial home of the Zaporozhian Cossacks, and where a Cossack museum hosts horsemanship shows.

As the river drifts south the weather warms and the fields are rich in corn and fruit. The small, but important, port city of Kherson, founded in 1778 by Catherine the Great, was named after the nearby Greek colony Chersonesos Taurica. St Catherine's Cathedral has the tomb of Prince Grigory Potemkin, the Russian military leader.

After Kherson the river again fragments into channels and islands for its final push into the Black Sea. Marking its path is the fabulous Adziogol Lighthouse, a steel lattice structure built in 1911 and 211ft (64m) tall. Its island setting is open to visitors.

From here it's 75 miles (120km) hugging the coast to the grand seaside resort of Odessa but half is protected by a wooded headland and riverboats can make it, across the mouths of several other rivers, to this fitting finale to an Eastern European odyssey.

THE DOURO

A cruise where both sides are port

Below: Vineyards form orderly lines on the steep valley sides, dotted with red-roofed wine estates, as the river flows through

Known to lovers of cruises as Portugal's river, the Douro actually extends for more than half its length in Spain before flowing west across Portugal to the Atlantic Ocean. Cruises on the Douro do Portugal from edge to edge, starting at Porto and mostly finishing just across the Spanish border. And if ever there was a cruise meant for sitting on the top deck in a sun-lounger and watching the world go gently by, this is the one.

The Douro's total length is 560 miles (900km) but only the Portuguese section is navigable, and then not by big ships: river cruise ships for the Douro are built short and shallow to cope with the low waters and the narrow,

weaving course. There are also short Six Bridges cruises (passing under all the bridges that cross at Porto), as well as multi-night cruises on *Spirit of Chartwell*, a grand river barge that used to sail on the Thames and was refurbished for the Queen's Diamond Jubilee in 2012 when she was the monarch's carriage during the extravagant river procession.

Part of the Douro valley is known as Vinhateiro (wine-growing), and is UNESCO protected. The sun-drenched sides are covered in vineyards, many of them growing grapes to make the local port, the rich fortified wine that found fans around the world.

Barrels of wine were traditionally taken downriver from the estates – *quintas* – in *rabelos* (small, wooden, flat-bottomed boats) and then stored in cellars in Vila Nova de Gaia, across the river from Porto. The picturesque quaysides where the barrels were once unloaded now accommodate passengers as a number of the cruise ships from many major companies depart from here.

Porto is a grand sight, a world of red-roofed buildings lazing in the sun as little boats flit about and the gleaming, contemporary cruise ships come and go. The medieval Ribeira (riverside) district is full of cobbled streets lined with merchants' houses, bars and cafés.

The city is packed with sights such as the glorious 14th-century Church of São Francisco, Gothic on the outside and baroque within, the Palácio da Bolsa, a neoclassical 19th-century landmark and the grandiose 19th-century São Bento railway station with 20,000 ornate

Below: The cruise ship *Emerald Radiance* glides through the warm setting of Porto, with Dom Luís I Bridge in the distance

Above: The lofty Côa Museum, near Pocinho and the Spanish border, celebrates the region's paleolithic past - and has great views

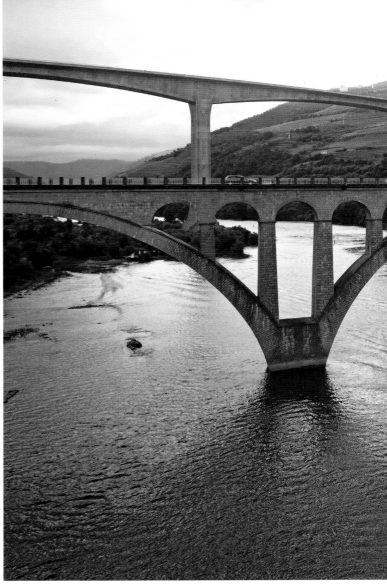

blue-and-white Mediterranean tiles from the early 20th-century decorating the main hall.

The most awe-inspiring sight in all of Porto is the towering, arched iron Dom Luís I Bridge, opened in 1887, which has a 1,296ft (395m) walkway along its 279ft (85m) high upper deck, connecting the hills that run along either side of the river – and giving extraordinary views over both the city and the Douro.

The river zig-zags even as it heads out of the ancient city, widening as the houses give way to greenery and it is barely several miles before the neat lines of vines that have been part of the landscape for so long start forming hypnotic patterns as they climb the hillsides.

There are dams, and locks, and camping grounds, and power stations, and beaches, and rural hotels as the Douro first heads south then twists north, then south again. The Tamega joins from the north with many cruises calling at little Entre-os-Rios just inside its mouth, the historic arched, concrete bridge reflecting perfectly in the still waters.

The river continues to twist and turn as it heads east. At Régua, on a picturesque bend, the lofty, modern Douro Museum opens the doors on the culture of this wine-rich region, showcasing the history of some of Portugal's greatest vineyards. Here, where brightly coloured buildings rise serenely up the banks, not one but two bridges leap the river — one with graceful arches, the other a startlingly high-level motorway crossing — the first for many miles.

By now you're in the area of the Varosa Valley, which runs just to the south, where, in the village of Tarouca, there's the splendid Monastery of Saint John of Tarouca. Here you can walk across the fortified stone bridge of Ucanha, Portugal's first toll bridge that crosses the Varosa River. It's around this point that cruises offer a tour to Mateus Palace, the place we're all so familar with from its

Above: *Scenic Azure* passes under the twin bridges of Régua surrounded, as is so much of the river, by vineyards

Left: Mateus Palace is a baroque fantasy, home to concerts and other events - but best known for its picture on the wine bottle

years of being featured on the labels of the famed Mateus rosé wine in its squat, curiously shaped bottles.

There are vineyards wherever you look in a landscape that verges on the arid yet is rich in its own way. It takes an entire day to pass through the Vinhateiro region. Recognised as a World Heritage Site, it has a history of wine production stretching back 2,000 years. Its port wine has been known around the world since the 18th century. The slopes here have a microclimate that, apart from grapes, olives and almonds thrive in, as seen in the huge orchards amid the vines.

The area around Pinhão and São João da Pesqueira is rated one of the best, with *quintas* commanding the steep slopes from which they produce the finest port. Pinhão is a charming little town with an arched stone bridge and ornately decorated railway station (on the scenic Douro Line) cosseted by the vineyard-covered hills.

Not far from the Spanish border is little, unhurried Pocinho, with its dam and locks. From here, tours often head to the Côa Valley Archaeological Park where, both along the Côa and along the Douro at more than 70 sites, are the biggest known collections of paleolithic open-air engravings. There is also the Côa Museum, a modern building high on the hillside, which offers interactive, digital scenes of the area – and fabulous river views. Pocinho is also the terminus of the Douro Line, the railway that runs from Porto, often seemingly close enough to the river to touch the water. Until the 1980s, when Spain closed its end, it ran across the border allowing travel to Salamanca.

Arriving at Vega de Terrón on the Spanish side is rather an anticlimax (border controls are dealt with onboard). The scenery is beautiful with low-lying hills drifting away into the distance, and you've finally reached Spain, and yet there's little here other than a dock where small pleasure craft moor alongside the sleek cruise ships… and a car park with buses waiting to transport you to Salamanca, one of the country's most historic cities.

But if you're on a cruise at least you are safe in the knowledge that your vessel will simply be turning around and you can enjoy all the scenery again in the other direction.

REIGN IN SPAIN

The Spanish end of the Douro is just as entrancing but very different, and not the place of cruise ships. The river emerges just north of the village of Duruelo de la Sierra, about 100 miles (160km) south of cosmopolitan Bilbao on the north-facing Atlantic coast. It crosses dusty mountains, entering the Cuerda del Pozo reservoir from the west and leaving in the east. This is a sunny spot with beaches, where you can swim and rent pedalos and other small boats, and where a drowned church tower still sticks its head above the water.

It becomes more river-like, dusty hillsides rising up around it, passing towns such as Soria, only about 25 miles (40km) from the lake, where it splashes over shallow rapids only a short walk from San Francisco de Asis, a grand church that was once part of a convent, and even a bull-ring. In Aranda de Duero, it is tree-lined and narrow, mostly languid although there are more rapids. Zamora is one of the most beautiful spots in the area, still nestling behind defensive walls with its cathedral (a Byzantine dome and Romanesque tower) rising from its hilltop setting. The river, still small and shallow, itself is fringed by greenery and has several little islands amongst several rocky rapids.

The Douro then forms the border between Spain and Portugal for 70 miles (112km), fighting its way through narrow, dusty canyons that still keep the two nations apart. Deep turquoise waters meander through the pale rock walls creating ever-changing vistas.

There are dams but even now bridges are few and far between. The isolated areas are protected – Douro International Natural Park on the Portuguese side, and Arribes del Duero Natural Park on the Spanish, stretching the length of the river border and farther. Small boats offer trips from the International Biology Station (a joint Portuguese and Spanish project) near Zamora. as the river snakes through the deep canyons.

Right: There are spectacular trips on little boats along the protected Douro canyon that divides Portugal and Spain

THE ELBE

A voyage the length of Germany

Right: The Bastei rock formation that towers above the Elbe and the dizzying stone bridge that dates from 1851

The Elbe starts in the Krkonoše Mountains in the north of the Czech Republic heading south, crossing the Bohemia region, making a big U-turn north of Prague and then flowing north-west across Germany, emptying into the sea at Cuxhaven, 70 miles (110km) from Hamburg. The river is, despite its somewhat discreet profile, one of Europe's big boys, linked by canals to Berlin and various industrial regions, and by the Elbe-Lübeck Canal to the Baltic Sea. The Kiel Canal, a short cut to the Baltic from the North Sea, starts near the river's mouth.

It's a river of two halves as far as cruises are concerned. There's the river from the German coast on the North Sea as far inland as the splendid seafaring city of Hamburg, a route taken by ocean cruise ships, not least the grandest of them all, *Queen Mary 2*. And then there's the inland section in which the river flows all the way across Germany

Left: The elegant waterfront of Dresden where cruise ships dock alongside exquisite baroque and renaissance architecture

Below: Meissen's Gothic Albrechtsburg castle with the spires of the cathedral rising behind

from its source deep in the Czech Republic. It's this Middle Europe area that crosses the border, verdant and picturesque, often untouched for centuries, that river cruises tend to celebrate.

River cruises often start in Děčín in Bohemia, some 60 miles (95km) north of Prague, at the Elbe's confluence with the Ploučnice. The pretty town is surrounded by low hills and its castle stands guard over the river. From here it is only a few miles to the German border and the state of Saxony. The river sweeps around the edge of the Saxon Switzerland National Park, where craggy sandstone bluffs rise up with forested peaks above. Next comes Bad Schandau, a delightful spa town with grand 19th-century

hotels lining the riverbank and a number of Renaissance buildings. Great river views can be had from the 173ft (52m) Bad Schandau Elevator, a fairytale-looking steel tower and lift, built in 1904, that connects the town with cliff-top Ostrau. Nearby the Bastei rock formation looms 636ft (194m) above the river – reached by a dizzying arched bridge, it is on most cruise tours.

The river, never wide but constantly navigable to small commercial vessels and many excursion ships, passes through the neat town of Pirna, then swiftly into the city of Dresden, a city known as the Florence of the Elbe for its baroque and renaissance architecture. Cruise ships dock in the middle of things.

Only a few miles farther is the town of Meissen, famed for its exquisite white porcelain since the 17th century – there's a tour of the factory, a museum and, of course, a shop. But the joy of Meissen is its hillside old town that pops up from the flatland, the spires of the cathedral looming over even the grandiose Albrechtsburg, the castle that is said to be Germany's oldest.

The Elbe then passes Riesa, with its Tierpark. The latter is a zoo in a monastery garden housing native creatures, such as the mouflon (a wild, horned mountain sheep), wild cats and storks. Next is Mühlberg, with its riverside lake.

The finale of most cruises is Wittenberg, the medieval town where in 1517 Martin Luther posted his *95 Theses*, a theological discussion that led to the Reformation. See Luther's House, St Marien's Church, where he preached,

and the castle church where he set the religious world alight. Historic buildings abound although the river is crossed by a twin road and rail bridge with gleaming arches, the contemporary design reflected in the calm waters and framed by the greenery along the banks.

The Elbe, however, continues for some 175 miles (280km) via the town of Magdeburg to Hamburg.

HAMBURG TO THE SEA

Hamburg is one of the great river cities, a grand medieval inland port watched over by the 433-ft (132m), copper-covered spire of St Michael's Church (open to the public and with sensational views). The wide city centre space of the old port is lined with elegant buildings, while the nearby historic waterfront warehouses now store restaurants and galleries. It is also host to the world's best port festival each May – more than 300 ships cluster around the waterfront, open for tours, offering trips and simply showing off in front of huge crowds. The weekend concludes with a vast procession along the river, often includ-

Above: Hamburg manages to be both a huge working port and an exquisite city with fascinating buildings and a splendid river festival

ing star guest *Queen Mary 2* or another Cunard ship.

The Old Elbe Tunnel, opened in 1911, was the continent's first river tunnel. Tiled and immaculate, with huge lift cages that will carry a car, the tunnel is free for pedestrians. This is a city of water, filled with hundreds of canals. And there are boats galore at any time of year, with harbour tours, some on barges, some that negotiate the canals, always dwarfed by the huge cruise and cargo ships.

The Elbe changes here, widening from a pretty inland waterway to something serious and wide. Leaving Hamburg involves sailing past the industrial area but more quickly than you'd imagine you're passing islands amid countryside and it's more than a mile from bank to bank.

Then it's a countryside idyll until you reach, on the right, the Kiel Canal. The locks (and museum) are a place to ship-watch as rugged vessels make their way between the gates. The river is all but over and opens into the North Sea.

THE GIRONDE AND THE DORDOGNE

From wide estuary to picturesque wine country

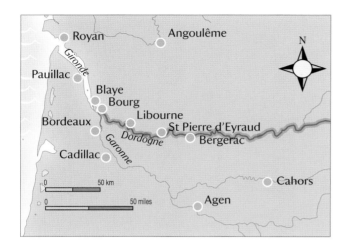

The Gironde, 50 miles (80km) long, is officially an estuary although often referred to as a river since it is a place of charming river cruises in the south-west of France. The confusion also comes from the fact that it is the outlet for two rivers, the Dordogne and the Garonne, which meet just above the elegant wine capital, Bordeaux, at the head of the estuary. This is an exquisitely mellow part of the country, where fertile rolling hills are often covered with vines as far as the eye can see, and the weather is warm and wonderful.

The Dordogne flows for some 300 miles (480km) before joining the Gironde. It starts more than 6,000ft (1,800m) up on Puy de Sancy, the highest peak in the Massif Central, from the coming together of two mountain streams, the Dore and the Dogne. Its westward path takes it through the Limousin and Périgord regions. The upper Dordogne takes its route from the mountains around it, a visually exciting mix of gorges with tall cliffs and vertigo-inducing bridges peppered with long, meandering lakes thanks to the five dams that corral the fast-flowing waters. It later widens into the dreamy landscape of the south-west, rich not just in vineyards but also in orchards, farmlands and pastures.

Stretches are open to pleasure boats but the river, once officially navigable all the way to the city of Bergerac, is now only open from Saint-Pierre-d'Eyraud, a few miles downstream from Bergerac and seven miles (12km)

Left: The scenery along the Dordogne starts to become more dramatic as the river meanders farther east

Above: Saint-Émilion is at the heart of some of France's most revered wine country with plenty of opportunities for tastings

upriver from the pretty town of Sainte-Foy-la-Grande. That only leaves a stretch of 75 miles (120km) of open river to where it meets the Garonne. The river here is much more conventional – less meandering and less prone to form channels and islands – than higher up.

River cruises (almost all multi-day cruises are return trips from Bordeaux) rarely head farther upstream than Libourne, only 30 miles (48m) from where the Dordogne and Garonne unite. The town is a lovely place to be, though, with architecture dating back to the 16th century. From here there's the prospect of a river excursion to the heart of Saint-Émilion wine country. These trips almost certainly include wine tastings at a château and a tour of the town, a UNESCO World Heritage Site, which sits on a hill a short distance upriver.

Just before the Dordogne and the Gironde meet, the village of Bourg, with its stone quay and clifftop houses is a regular cruise call, with a tour into Cognac country a tempting alternative to riverside relaxation.

The estuary is a different kettle of seafood, a body of water reaching seven miles (11km) wide yet protected by a mouth less than half that. Stops include Pauillac, a little town surrounded by the vineyards of Château Lafite Rothschild, Château Latour and Château Mouton Rothschild, whose estates pour down towards the water. Aside from all the pleasure craft, you're as likely to see barges carrying Airbus A380 wings from the dock (where they arrive from the UK and Germany) to the other side of Bordeaux (where they are transferred by road for assembly near Toulouse). Across the water is Blaye where a sprawling citadel encompasses a medieval castle, which, along with the city walls and varied other forts, are UNESCO protected.

You'll know you've reached the sea when you arrive at the resort town of Royan with its south-facing beach, promenade and Belle Epoque houses. Take a long look back from the little Bac Royan-Pointe de Grave ferry that crosses the estuary mouth, passing the Cordouan Lighthouse that sits imperiously on its own island.

THE GIRONDE AND THE GARONNE
The spirit of western France

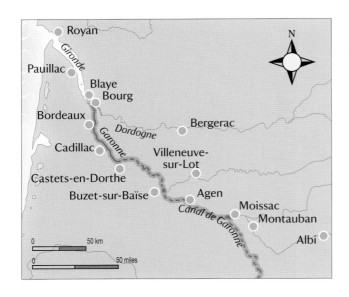

Right: Pont Saint-Pierre in the heart of Toulouse with the grand dome of the Hôpital La Grave dominating the skyline

The Garonne is the second of two rivers (the other is the Dordogne, pages 40–41) that unite near Bordeaux to create the Gironde Estuary. But whereas the Dordogne travels down from the French Alps in a south-westerly direction, the Garonne emerges in the Spanish Pyrenees and flows north. From its source some 6,000ft (1,800m) up in the Aran Valley (although the exact spot is the subject of much discussion), it tumbles down mountain slopes and then passes through the cities of Toulouse and Agen.

Ocean vessels, including moderate-sized cruise ships can sail up the Gironde and into the Garonne for a short stretch, docking in Bordeaux. The city straddles a river bend, the right bank to the east and the more developed left bank in the west. It's a delicate, exquisite place to arrive at, halting near Pont de Pierre (stone bridge). The city is a UNESCO World Heritage Site with more protected buildings than anywhere in France outside Paris. Yet it also has extraordinary modern architecture such as the

riverside La Cité du Vin, a homage to the grape, and Pont Jacques Chaban-Delmas, a 2013 lift bridge whose central section rises 250ft (75m) to let ships pass.

Inland vessels such as river cruise ships can sail 50 miles (80km) farther to the little town of Castets-en-Dorthe. From here the 19th-century Canal de Garonne makes it possible, via more than 50 locks, for shipping to avoid the shimmying on the river itself and reach Toulouse. It also forms part of the Canal des Deux Mers, linking Mediterranean and Atlantic. Boat excursions in Toulouse often venture on to the next stretch, the Canal du Midi.

Toulouse is a pretty place, known as the Pink City for the large number of terracotta-huded buildings. The river splits into two main channels around a collection of islands full of parks and amenities.

The cruise from Bordeaux to Castets-en-Dorthe might be short yet it is what south-west France is all about. Few things are more beautiful than following the river as it weaves through the rolling countryside under the warm sun. Most cruises call at Cadillac, about half way to Castets-en-Dorthe. The little port dates back to the 13th century and is across the river from the Sauternes wine region — the town is known for its sweet dessert wines and, like so many places in this region, there are places for tastings.

River cruises almost always take in the Garonne as part of a week-long trip that also wanders into the Dordogne and explores the towns of the Gironde Estuary. Smaller pleasure boats head farther up the Garonne. The Garonne, like the Dordogne, has a tidal bore, a strong wave that rolls up the river, so you can expect to see surfers and jet skiers amongst the pleasure craft and small fishing boats.

In Bordeaux there are short boat trips up and down the city, under its seven bridges, one, of course, involving wine tasting. Speedboat rides, outings on the listed sailing ship *l'Arawak* and more are also on offer either heading upstream on a laid-back river through idyllic countryside or downstream into the sea-like estuary.

THE GUADALQUIVIR

Spain's only great navigable river

Below: The elegant Triana Bridge in Seville, dating from 1852, is a place to cross between the lively riverbanks on an evening stroll

It's a mesmerising sight. The Triana Bridge, with its elegant iron flourishes, arches its way across the river, illuminated by spotlights in the warm evening. The tree-lined banks are alive with chatter as people walk happily, calling at open-air bars and restaurants that are creating paella from local seafood.

Seville is a romantic place sitting on two Guadalquivirs, the main channel that runs along the city's eastern edge and the wide, canal-like leg that protrudes into the main part. The latter is entered through a lock and at first you think you're simply in the docks (said to be Spain's only river port) but after rounding a bend you find yourself in a tree-lined paradise, a classical river scene filled with the sultry charm of Spain.

Swathed in sun, the city is a gem that marks the limit of navigation on a river that flows 400 miles (640km) from the mountains down through Córdoba, entering the Atlantic just north of the port of Cádiz. Seville is only 50 miles (80km) from the sea; in Roman times the river was navigable to Córdoba, another 80 miles (130km) but dams now make that impossible. It is still, however, Spain's only seriously navigable river.

The stretch from Seville to the sea may be short yet it is a dream-like journey through the countryside of Andalucía, a world where flamenco and fine foods go hand in hand.

And because Seville is a port town, it's possible for smaller ocean cruise ships to sail in from the sea as well as for river cruise ships to offer round trips. The banks of the Guadalquivir's offshoot are full of riverboats, from regular tourist vessels to little, silent electrically-propelled craft, offering sightseeing trips under the city's varied bridges and past its ornate and ancient buildings such as the Torre del Oro, a 13th-century military watchtower still looking over the waters.

The city is lovely in itself yet set sail from the heart of Seville on a week-long river cruise and you're quickly into well-tended farmland mixed with pastures where cattle just stand and watch. The simplicity doesn't last long as before you know it the town of Coria del Río springs up on the western bank. There's a neat riverfront path and a tiny flatbed car ferry criss-crossing the river, which is only a few hundred feet wide at this point.

A few miles later the Guadaira river joins from the north-east. A couple of miles down from the confluence a channel forks off to the left and forms its own river as it heads through Brazo del Este Natural Park. There are 25 miles (40km) of bends until it rejoins the Guadalquivir, only 10 miles (16km) from where it branched off.

The park is a wetland site, where red eucalyptus trees proliferate and thousands of birds, from purple herons to waterfowl and birds of prey, live. It's never more than a mile or two from the main river and the peace and quiet reaches across.

Go only a short distance farther and you're in Doñana National Park which dwarfs the Brazo. For the final 20 miles (32km) the river passes and ducks through the vast area of marshes, streams and dunes that is part of the Guadalquivir River Delta.

Designated by UNESCO as both a World Heritage Site and a Biosphere Reserve, this is a wild place of big skies where the wildlife is extraordinarily varied for a coastal preserve: apart from the thousands of birds that swoop and rise, there are wild boar, deer, otters, wild horses, even endangered species such as the Iberian Lynx and Spanish Imperial Eagle.

Just as the river comes to the end of the park it gives a sharp turn southward and passes the seaside resort and

Below: Cádiz, an enticing city with beaches, markets and shops, sits on the Mediterranean near the mouth of the Guadalquivir

Bottom: The dunes and marshes of Doñana National Park, near where the river meets the sea, are home to lynx and wild boar

fishing town of Sanlúcar de Barrameda. This is suddenly a different world, one of big family beaches, and shops and bars. Less than 15 miles (25km) down the coast and you're in the Bay of Cádiz.

River cruises tend to dock at El Puerto de Santa María, a couple of miles before the city of Cádiz, with its Castillo san Marcos fortification, domed cathedral, little Guadalete river and varied beaches.

Cádiz itself is lovely, filled with little streets, smart shops, markets and beaches. This is a regular stop for ocean cruise ships and is likely to feature on any ocean itinerary that also takes in Seville.

The journey to and from Seville is a very different experience depending on the size of ship – river ships sink into the landscape, cosseted by the tree-lined banks, while ocean vessels rise above the plains of Spain giving panoramic views into the distance.

A CITY CAST ADRIFT

While Córdoba can now only be reached by road, given the shallow waters of the Guadalquivir here, it is a gorgeous riverside destination. It owes its stately elegance to the Romans who filled it with memories, not least the exquisite arched Roman bridge dating from the 1st century BC. Other relics include a temple, mausoleum and forum.

History reveals itself with a number of water-powered flourmills from the Moorish era. A couple of thousand years ago the river was navigable to the sea and made Córdoba an important city for trade and transport. Water barely flows under the Roman bridge these days but you can get a feel for the place by walking across it, now open only to pedestrians and cyclists, not even a chariot...

Below: Córdoba's Roman bridge dates from the 1st century when the now shallow river was an important waterway all the way to the sea

THE MAIN

A Rhine tributary yet still a Main attraction

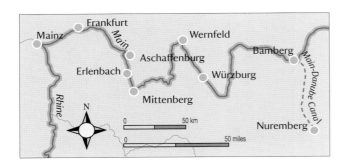

Below: The glass towers of Frankfurt provide a stirring contrast to the green and pleasant riverside path

A major river in itself although still very much known as a tributary of the Rhine, the Main lies entirely in Germany, the longest river that does so. It starts in pretty, chocolate-box Bavaria, on the south-west edge of the town of Kulmbach, under the watchful eye of hilltop Plassenburg Castle. The town welcomes the Main's sources, each around 30 miles (50km) long, the White Main (from the Fichtel mountains that spill into the Czech Republic) and

the Red Main (from the Jura mountains), which come together in less than dramatic fashion in the countryside.

The Main then flows for 325 miles (520km), all the way to the Rhine across from the city of Mainz, visiting quaint towns such as Bamberg and Würzburg as well as the high-rise city of Frankfurt as it makes its way.

The Main is navigable to modest vessels from the Rhine all the way to Bamberg, a distance of around 250 miles

(400km), taking in 34 dams and their locks. It is this journey that is offered by many of the major cruise companies, although the itineraries often throw in the Rhine and even the Danube, to which the Main is also connected via the 105-mile (170km) Main-Danube Canal, a waterway that runs from Bamberg to Kelheim via Nuremberg.

A cruise along the Main is very much a journey to the heart of Germany, with medieval buildings, ornate church spires and timeless scenery. And Bamberg is very much a river town; it's here that the waters of the Regnitz join the Main from the south and with the medieval, half-timbered town hall sitting on an island in the former. It's a beautiful place, set across seven gentle hills with the 1,000-year-old Romanesque cathedral's four towers an unmistakable landmark no matter which direction you're coming from.

The Main leaves a mosaic of countryside lakes in its wake as it leaves town, then even more lakes as it drifts through a placid region of farmland formed into neat fields. It passes through towns such as Schweinfurt (it translates as 'swine ford'), with its Renaissance town hall and riverside park, before turning south and executing a hairpin bend in the town of Volkach, an area rich in vineyards.

Würzburg is unmistakable, dominated by the imposing and elegant Fortress Marienberg that looks down from its hillside pedestal. Church spires dot the roofscape, packed with Baroque and Rococo architecture, not least the truly huge UNESCO-protected Residenz Palace.

By this stage the river is heading north again, but only for a short while before one more about turn to Miltenberg. This is another medieval treasure, wedged between the river and slopes of the Odenwald mountain, with around 150 half-timbered houses still standing in its romantic old town along with Hotel Zum Riesen, possibly the country's oldest inn.

Passing through wine country where neat vines line the hills, it's not long before another change of direction as the river passes through Aschaffenburg where it's impossible to miss the riverside Schloss Johannisburg, a Renaissance palace dating back to the early 17th century. Huge, square and built of red sandstone with a turret on each corner, it was a home of the Prince Bishop of Mainz. The river here is on a bend and has formed itself into twin channels sandwiching a long, narrow, tree-covered island.

Then it is quickly on to Frankfurt, a city where glass towers mingle with imposing historic buildings and tree-lined riverbanks offer lovely places to stroll. The 850ft (259m) Commerzbank Tower is Germany's tallest building and for a number of years, until pipped by one in Moscow, was the tallest in Europe. It is one of many (earning the city the name Mainhattan) that reflect beautifully in the river when illuminated at night. They gaze over the Wallanlagen, a park that follows the ancient city walls, dropping down to the edge of the river. In Frankfurt you'll find a number of boat excursions from a number of local companies, from short sightseeing trips through the city, to dinner cruises, to day trips that take you down and on to the Rhine.

From Frankfurt it is barely 30 miles (50km) to the Rhine, where the Main pours out opposite Mainz old town. This is a city to enjoy, with relaxed riverside paths as well as places such as the Gutenberg Museum, home to the earliest printed Bibles, and imposing St Martin's Cathedral. Mainz is a major port, the Rhine connecting with the Neckar, the Main and Moselle to the bulk of continental Europe and, via Rotterdam, the North Sea. The Museum of Ancient Seafaring testifies to the city's importance, celebrating the Roman vessels that were found here.

The Main might end here but for many cruises this is simply a call on a longer voyage that takes in at least one more river as it navigates through the heart of Europe.

Right: Schloss Johannisburg on the Main in rural Aschaffenburg, 17th-century home of the Prince Bishop of Mainz

THE MARNE
Water with bubbles in it

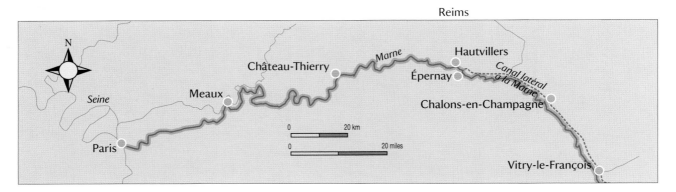

This is Champagne cruising on a stretch of river that's short but sweet – although not too sweet, obviously. The Marne is a tributary of the Seine in eastern France, running 320 miles (515km) from the limestone Langres Plateau, ending by snaking through the suburbs of southern Paris and joining the Seine only five miles (8km) south-east of Notre Dame cathedral.

The Marne is a gentle river that doesn't open itself up to major cruises but small boats, holiday barges and hotel barges enjoy the relaxed pace, particularly the stretch between Meaux, the first major town east of Paris, and Châlons-en-Champagne, passing through protected lands south of the city of Reims.

Meaux is a classically understated French place, its Romanesque cathedral standing tall over the river, which flows under stone bridges, even past a little beach, and performs a hairpin turn in the middle of the town.

The Marne continues to meander through charmingly French countryside dotted with little riverside communes, not least Château-Thierry, which curiously doesn't have a château but is an idyllic town amongst the rolling hills. Nearby is Belleau Wood, scene of a major 1918 battle when British, American and French united in a decisive push against the Germans; the American cemetery alongside contains the graves of almost 2,500 US soldiers.

We're now entering Champagne country proper and the town of Hautvillers, where the Abbey of Saint Peter was the home of Dom Pérignon, the Benedictine monk whose fermentations are said to have put the sparkle into wine. His resting place is at what remains of the abbey, a five-minute walk from the river.

Hautvillers is on the Marne itself but it is between here and the village of Dizy barely a mile away that the Canal Latéral de la Marne starts, a 40-mile (75km) waterway to Vitry-le-François built to cut out the relentless bends of the Marne (which continues to splash along happily beside it). From Hautvillers, most barge cruises take the simple way out, the Marne itself simply taking too long and being barely navigable in places.

Across both river and canal from Dizy is Epernay which positively bubbles with Champagne houses – the vast home of Moët et Chandon along with names such as Gosset, Pol Roger and Mercier, all open for tours and tastings (and buyings).

Vineyards (Veuve Clicquot, Mumm, among a number of others) cloak the surrounding hills as the canal slides through Montagne de Reims regional park (a protected area of hills cloaked with Champagne vineyards), with Reims 15 miles (24km) to the north. Barges glide along with guests sometimes choosing to stroll along the towpath but more often to sit on deck sampling a glass of the local bubbly.

Châlons-en-Champagne, much smaller than Reims is nevertheless the region's capital (only renamed from

Châlons-sur-Marne in 1998 after, one imagines, the burghers had sat down one evening with a glass or two). Here the river is on the straight and narrow, passing through the town parallel to the canal several minutes walk away.

A separate, short stretch of canal (Canal Saint-Martin) leaves the river and cuts through the old town, passing classical architecture such as the twin cathedrals of Notre-Dame-en-Vaux (a UNESCO-protected building) and Saint-Étienne (a Romanesque/Gothic/Baroque mixture) before joining the main canal.

The Marne starts to wriggle again after leaving town and the canal makes it a few more miles before a T-junction with the Marne-Rhine to the left (heading for Strasbourg) and Canal Entre Champagne et Bourgogne (connecting with Maxilly-sur-Saône to the north of Lyon).

Top: The Abbey of St Peter, Hautvillers, where Dom Pérignon worked his magic on wine and is buried in the little cemetery

Above: The Marne is a tranquil river to travel, with the temptation to stop and sample another variety of Champagne

THE MOSELLE

Wine and the sweetest of scenery

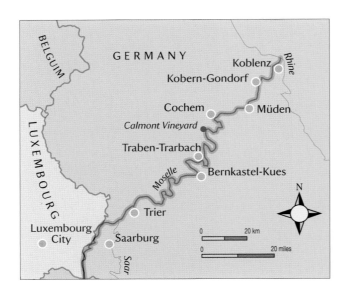

Right: Reichsburg Castle gazes over Cochem, one of the river's most serene and beautiful towns, from its hilltop setting

There's a point, at Koblenz, where the Moselle and Rhine meet, that is one of the most dramatic on Europe's rivers. The twin waterways come together at a sharp point, where an enormous statue of Kaiser Wilhelm I on his horse looks up at the lofty buildings on the opposite bank. It's the Rhine that gets all the attention, the big brother of the two, but the Moselle (often called the Mosel in Germany), in its own genteel way, is nevertheless a river that resonates with the continent's history and beauty.

It all starts 340 miles (550km) back, some 2,400ft (750m) up on the Ballon d'Alsace peak in the Vosges Mountains in France. The extremely meandering Moselle Valley then offers different takes on the heart of Europe at every turn – and there are many. The river flows through France's Lorraine region and little Luxembourg then into Germany (at first forming the Luxembourg-Germany border) to a world of hills, vineyards and crumbling castles. In its early stages, the land beside the river is busy with

industry, including mining and steel-making, but once past Trier the bends and hillsides are just too much for over-development – although the bends don't prevent the river being widely used by commercial barges.

Many cruise trips start from Trier, about 30 miles (48km) north-east of Luxembourg City and just after the River Saar has poured in. Trier, founded by the Romans is full of monuments and relics from the empire – not least the Porta Nigra gate, amphitheatre and the late 19th century stone bridge over the Moselle itself.

The river now flows through the Moselle wine region, between the low mountain ranges of the Eifel to the north and Hunsrück in the south, and the hills are blanketed with vines while the riverbanks give way to Kenner Flur, a nature reserve on a floodplain in a large bend that is home to geese and many other birds.

Despite the river's twists and turns, it is a busy waterway with cargo vessels outnumbering the sleek cruise ships – a

large number of locks keep things in motion since the river was upgraded in the 1960s, with cargo ships able to get upriver almost to Nancy in France. Yet the modern world doesn't push aside the fairytale landscape: at Bernkastel-Kues the river does a hairpin turn around the town. This charming medieval town has a lovely market square and a ruined castle with ramparts that give enchanting views of the river from the outside of the bend.

Traben-Trarbach is another pretty town on a bend, the Germanic Art Nouveau-style of the turreted Brückentor gatehouse to the river bridge connecting two parts of town, setting the tone. Traben wanders along the left bank while Trarbach stretches away between the peaks of the Kautenbach valley on the right.

At Pünderich the looping turn is so tight that the parts of the river are separated by only a few hundred feet. Cochem, perhaps the river's most enchanting town, sits beneath steeply rising hills with 1,000-year-old Reichsburg

Castle on its own hilltop. Tours on cruises head off to castles, and to vineyards for tastings of the Riesling that makes the region so famous.

Several of the vineyards were started in medieval times by monks, and they're still going today. Wines tend to be sold locally. The vineyards and the castles can all be seen from on high thanks to the Moselle Ridgeway, established more than a century ago, a walking trail running for 165 miles (260km) on the Hunsrück side and 115 miles (185km) on the Eifel side. There's also plenty of opportunity to walk or cycle on paths along the river itself.

Farther along, at Müden, Eltz Castle, like something from a storybook, sits on a rocky outcrop among tree-covered hills with the Elzbach River gurgling around it on several sides before it drops into the Moselle.

The Moselle narrows as it approaches Koblenz, passing under several bridges (historic Balduinbrücke giving neat views over town and Rhine beyond) before the confluence

at Deutsches Eck (German Corner) where it flows into the Rhine and where the 121ft (37m) tall monument to Kaiser Wilhelm I stands. For some, this is as far as it goes although many river cruises combine the Moselle (sometimes simply the stretch as far as Bernkastel) with a classic stretch of the Rhine.

Koblenz is a splendid town with churches and cobble-stone streets, footpaths along the Moselle and a change of scale as you walk in a loop and emerge on the banks of the Rhine. Close by Deutsches Eck a cable car lifts visitors across the Rhine up to Ehrenbreitstein Fortress on its rocky plateau for the best views of all, taking in both rivers and myriad bridges.

TAKE A SIP
There are plenty of vineyards along the Moselle Valley, most of them facing south or south-west on the

Above: The Moselle, straight ahead, meets the Rhine at Deutches Eck, under the huge statue of Kaiser Wilhelm 1

Right: Luxury cruise ship *Scenic Jasper* glides past the wine-growing hillsides of Bremm in the golden, late-summer sun

often-steep hillsides that rise up from the river. A gradient of 60 per cent isn't uncommon while the Calmont vine-yard at Bremm, a short distance east of Cochem, is reck-oned the steepest in Europe at 68 per cent. The richest stretches are from Trier to Koblenz and Bernkastel-Kues to Cochem. Even the smallest villages have festivals to cele-brate the year's new product, a highlight in the late sum-mer and autumn — and the later it gets, the more the weather mellows. Bernkastel-Kues is the undisputed heart of the Middle Moselle's wine-growing area and with its medieval market place and grand, half-timbered buildings is a lovely place to celebrate the harvest.

THE PO

A taste of Italy with the style of Venice

In a country not known for its big rivers, the Po makes its mark yet still manages to slip under the radar for many. It cuts across northern Italy for 400 miles (640km), from the southern Alps (on the slopes of Monte Viso, highest mountain of the Cottian Alps), flowing through Turin before arriving just outside Venice. The river ends in a sweeping delta that covers much of the Venice area, the waters reaching the sea and Venice Lagoon by a number of paths.

The Po Valley is wide and graceful, a place inhabited for millions of years, not least during the Roman Empire, and the journey here is through the laid-back scenery of southern Europe, a landscape dotted with ancient churches. The Po isn't a major river as they go and is certainly not open to major navigation. River cruises usually head from Venice itself to Polesella, taking in only about 40 miles (60km) of the river. Smaller boats such as holiday barges can make it another 60 or so miles (100km) to the city of Mantua.

Cruises start in the city and begin by journeying the canals. The Grand Canal is magical with its Bridge of Sighs and St Mark's Basilica, which is romantically lit in the evening. Heading from Venice, cruises pass through the lagoon, one of the most staggeringly beautiful sights on the world's waters – often with the chance of finding yourself

dwarfed by an ocean cruise ship – past the Lido, the narrow island of Pellestrina with its flamboyantly painted fishermen's houses and the huge MOSE flood-control project. Cruises often visit islands in the lagoon such as Murano, famed for its glass-making.

The Po Delta itself, outside the city, is a land of salt marshes where flamingos and herons enjoy the sun and the warm breeze. The Venetian Delta Regional Park swathes the entrance to the river in grassy greenery. Walks in the park give views of little islands.

First call is Chioggia, often called Little Venice, at the southern end of the lagoon, a place of beaches and marinas just before the river's mouth.

Once in the river, Taglio Di Pô is a pretty holiday town set in a flat green landscape. It has a riverside promenade, and smart restaurants and shops. The onward journey is uneventful in the best kind of way, gentle farmland and rolling hills, vineyards and villages all the way to Polesella, which is just as unassuming. The little town is a lovely place to stroll, gazing at the 16th-century Palazzo Grimani and the 17th-century Villa Morosini, or wandering amidst the low, wild greenery of the riverbanks.

If you're on a barge, the next stretch is perhaps the more interesting, the river narrowing and occasionally dividing

into two or more channels. At Mantua the river turns away south and its tributary, the Mincio, joins it from the heart of town. In the town itself the Mincio forms a giant lake around the town's headland where churches and classical buildings form an entrancing roofscape. There are local boat trips available on the Mincio.

The Po, meanwhile, slips away all but unnoticed, becoming a pleasing country river that wanders through lovely towns such as Piacenza before entering the greenery of the discreet Po Valley itself, eventually finding itself at the heart of Turin.

In the city the river flows under classical bridges, such as Ponte Isabella, and past grand buildings, parks and gardens, with the Alps rising gently on the horizon. From here the river is narrower as it flows from the mountains.

Above: European Waterways' *La Bella Vita*, a 'hotel barge' for only 20 passengers, in Mantua, the farthest point it reaches from Venice

Right: Cruises along the Po start out on the canals of Venice – although perhaps not canals as small as this

THE RHINE
AMSTERDAM TO MAINZ
From the North Sea all the way to Germany

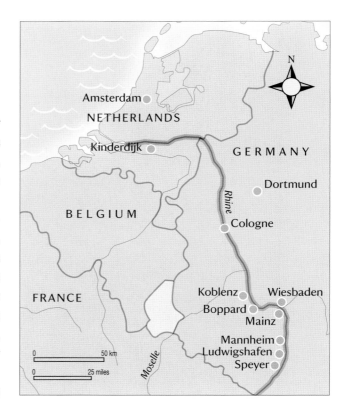

The Rhine is Europe's longest river and has been a major trade route since ancient times. It flows from the Swiss Alps through Switzerland, Liechtenstein, Austria, Germany, France and the Netherlands to the North Sea and creates a natural border for some of these countries.

It was the Romans who first used the Rhine as a super-highway to access the territories they ruled and now, when you take a cruise along any part of the 766 miles (1,232km), you are time-travelling through Europe. The section from Amsterdam in the Netherlands to Mainz in Germany is the busiest because it can be seen easily in a simple seven-day cruise. As well as week-long cruises, there are plenty of other trips, from half-days to two or three days.

A day spent in Amsterdam is always rewarding. There are galleries full of paintings, such as the Van Gogh Museum that contains some of the Dutch painter's finest works, while the city's Jewish history is also fascinating: book online if you want to visit Anne Frank's House as the queues are ever-present. Head, too, for the Jewish Historical Museum in the heart of the former Jewish quarter. Here there are four historic synagogues, including the 17th-century Portuguese Synagogue with its UNESCO-listed library.

But if you just want to get to the heart of what Amsterdam is all about, take a stroll amongst the canals to see how people still live and work along these extraordinary feats of engineering – a canal boat ride through the maze is hypnotic.

Cruises tend to sail from Amsterdam's big internal waterfront, right by the station and a ferry-ride away from the modernistic EYE Filmmuseum. Given that the Rhine splinters into a delta near the coast, the first stretch is generally along the River Ijssel, a branch of the Rhine and part of the city's canal system that leads from Ijsselmeer, the closed-off bay that shelters the city. The river joins the

Right: Amsterdam's waterfront houses come in a wild variety of designs and are full of restaurants and shops

Below: Cologne's cathedral is visible from almost everywhere in the city, not least the river as cruise ships pass by

Nederrijn south of the city of Arnhem which itself joins up with the Rhine a few miles later.

This being the Netherlands, the landscape tends to be flat, with neat towns and well-irrigated farmland amidst the lakes that dot the floodplains.

Entering Germany, the first major stop is Cologne, where the cathedral is a five-minute walk from the river and impossible to miss: it's northern Europe's largest Gothic church. These days you have to pay to get more than a glimpse inside this symbol of Germany's post-war rebirth. Among its treasures is the 12th-century solid gold shrine of the Three Kings who attended Jesus' birth, built to hold what are claimed to be their bones. A Roman floor, the Dionysos Mosaic, discovered beside the cathedral while an air raid shelter was being dug during the Second World War, is now in the museum next door.

Much of Cologne was rebuilt in the 1960s, with architecture to match, but the Old Town was carefully reconstructed and can be found on Altstadt between Gross St Martin Church and the Deutzer Bridge. The Old Town is the setting for the most magical Christmas market in Cologne, of which there are several — including four around the cathedral. For those culturally inclined, one of the best attractions is Museum Ludwig, full of modern art from Kandinsky, Picasso, Dali and Klee – plus American pop art — and there is plenty of evidence of the 1st-century Roman settlement, such as the Praetorium foundations under the city hall and the Romisch-Germanisches Museum that tells the history of the Romans along the Rhine. It's where the Dionysos mosaic floor is now on display.

This northern stretch of the Rhine, where working barges occupy the waters along with many cruise ships, is deep within Germany's wine country, as you soon discover in Koblenz. Strategically placed where the Rhine meets the Moselle, Koblenz straddles the river and has been a wine merchants' town for centuries. There is a weindorf (wine village) in the town built for a 1920s wine fair. Its scenic taverns are worth visiting for a glass or two, and if you are lucky you might be able to take part in one of its regular events. The Old Town is near the 14th-century Balduinbrücke (Balduin Bridge), although few old buildings survived the Second World War and the bridge itself had to be rebuilt.

Fairytale castles, or at least elaborate fortresses, stand guard over the river, with Ehrenbreitstein the second-largest historic fortress in Europe. Like most castles along this river, it stands high in the cliffs — as does Stolzenfels Castle with its castellated towers and curtain-like walls, which is up in the mountains surrounded by forest.

South from Koblenz you drift through the UNESCO-listed Rhine Gorge, 40 miles (65km) of dramatic cliffs and thickly forested hillsides plus steeply terraced vineyards, that continues almost to Mainz.

You'll sail past the mysterious rocks of Lorelei on a bend with Castle Katz looking down as your ship navigates one of the trickiest sections of the river. Legend has it that

boats were shipwrecked here lured by the sight of Lorelei, a beautiful woman sitting on a rock combing her golden hair, who threw herself to her death while she was being taken to a convent, away from the man she loved.

Boppard, south of Rhens, is the starting point for many cruise trips, as the river is only a few hundred yards from the railway station, and another pretty place for a brief visit. It has a few Roman ruins, including sections of 2,000-year-old walls, while the fortress Kurtrierische Burg, on the riverbank, is the town's museum.

Many of the picturesque forts on the Middle Rhine from Koblenz to Rüdesheim were restored in the 1800s when steamboats transformed the river into a tourist attraction. Rüdesheim is one of the cheeriest stops. First settled by the Celts and then the Romans in the 1st century, it once belonged to the 13th-century knights of Rüdesheim and retains a medieval feel with cobbled streets and half-timbered buildings. The most famous street is Drosselgasse, more of a wide alley really, lined with wine bars and taverns that look like they might have come from a Brothers

Opposite: The town of Sankt Goarshausen, topped by Katz Castle, just north of the rocks of Lorelei in the Rhine Gorge

Above: *Viking Mani* is one of the many contemporary cruise ships on the river, contrasting to the Rhine's historic setting

Grimm fairytale – the coloured glass windows and heavy wooden interiors are straight out of the Seven Dwarves' house.

Several of these old streets are filled with Christmas market stalls during December, and the knights' castle is now the Bromersburg Wine Museum. But the town's most unusual year-round attraction is Siegreid's Mechanical Music Museum, a collection of automated musical instruments from around Germany.

Smaller towns include Bacharach, named after the god of wine, Bacchus. It is home to the second oldest wine tavern in Germany, a half-timbered and turreted building called Altes Haus (Old House) with the date of its origin – 1368 – on its wall. Bacharach is not as touristy as Rüdesheim and some would say that makes it even more charming. It

was certainly popular during the 19th-century Age of Romanticism, mainly thanks to the ruins of a Gothic-style chapel that was never completed but attracted artistic types lucky enough to be on a Grand Tour of Europe.

But it's Mainz that is the finale in the Middle Rhine. Its strategic position where the Rhine meets the Main is to thank for its role as capital of Germany's federal state of Rhineland-Palatinate, not to mention its reputation as Germany's wine capital. Mainz holds a wine fair every August – Weinmarkt – when there are stalls selling not only wine but also food, and arts and crafts. There are also lots of musical performances in parks and open spaces.

Year-round attractions include 12th-century Mainz Cathedral, one of the most important in Germany. It's at the heart of the maze of medieval lanes full of the region's typical half-timbered buildings that house cafés, boutiques and, of course, wine bars. Also impressive is St Stephan Kirche, a Gothic parish church that was rebuilt after the Second World War and now has nine windows by Russian artist Marc Chagall in his characteristic brilliant colours that make the soul soar.

Mainz's most important cultural attraction, though, is the Gutenberg Museum, which traces the history of the written word and most importantly the first printing press set up in Mainz in 1446 by goldsmith Johann Gutenberg. The Gutenberg Bible was the first printed Bible and it's no exaggeration to say it changed the world. Three of Gutenberg's original Bibles are on display in a vault-like room with thick iron doors.

Outside there's a tree-lined riverside walk in one direction, the cathedral across the traffic-free precinct in the other, and a narrow, shop- and café-filled main street in what might be a city but which has the feel of a market town. The Rhine, however, continues on its next stretch...

Left: Mainz Cathedral, just off the waterfront, rises grandly from the cityscape and is visible from a great distance along the river

THE RHINE
MAINZ TO BASEL
A voyage across the heart of Europe

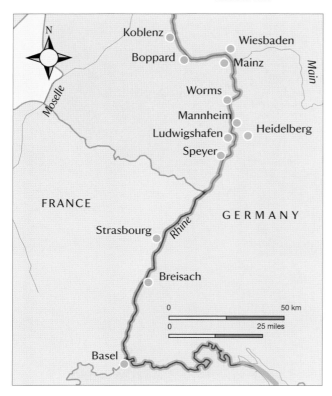

The Upper Rhine leaves Mainz in Germany and heads for Basel in Switzerland, a stretch used for many a cruise, with highlights including the French cathedral city of Strasbourg and the older section of Basel, with its ancient Germanic feel. Few mainstream cruise lines venture further south than Basel, as in this section from its source high up in the mountains of Gotthard Massif in south-east Switzerland the Rhine is busy plunging past Alpine villages.

It's because the upper Rhine is relatively short that it often forms just a part of cruises that start all the way from Amsterdam in the Netherlands and run through Germany to Cologne and Mainz before the final stretch in France and Switzerland. However, one- or two-night trips can sometimes be taken between Strasbourg and Basel, with the only other main stop in that section being the Alsace town of Breisach on the edge of the Black Forest in Germany, about 37 miles (60km) from Basel.

After leaving Mainz, regarded as the capital of German wine, the river takes you down to Worms, one of Germany's oldest towns and an important administrative centre

during the Holy Roman Empire, from 1034 to 1806. The Empire was closely allied to the Catholic Church and it was here, in 1521, that Dr Martin Luther presented his Protestant doctrine to the assembly – or Diet – and Emperor Charles V.

The town became Protestant in 1525 and a massive monument to Luther and the Protestant Reformation is now one of the town's most significant sights. But the town is also surrounded by vineyards and the wine trade remains a dominant force here. In fact, the white wine that became so popular in the 1970s – Liebfraumilch – is named after the Liebfrauenstift convent in Worms and produced in the surrounding vineyards.

It is possible to take a day-trip cruise on the River Neckar from Worms to Heidelberg, best known for being the home of Germany's oldest university. The 1924 film *The Student Prince* featuring the famous "Drinking Song" was set here and its ruined castle is one of the most important

Left: The vast riverfront Rhein-Galerie collection of shops and restaurants on the site of an old harbour in Ludwigshafen

Above: The city of Speyer and its unusual, four-towered cathedral, the burial place of German emperors for almost 300 years

Renaissance buildings in northern Europe. Walk up the hill or take the funicular for fabulous views over city and river.

Day trips to Worms and Heidelberg are also available from Mannheim, where the Neckar joins the Rhine. Mannheim has been an important industrial town since a two-wheel Laufmaschine, the precursor to the bicycle, was built here in 1817. Mercedes-Benz and Daimler cars were originally based here, too, and that's reflected in Mannheim's technology museum – Technoseum – while the city's wealth is to thank for the Kunsthalle Mannheim art museum, which in 2017 had a superb glass extension added to the original Art Nouveau building from the International Art Exhibition of 1907.

Opposite Mannheim is Ludwigshafen, an industrialised city that, like Mannheim, was bombed during the Second World War. Both rebuilt themselves: Mannheim reconstructing its Baroque Mannheim Palace, which has some rooms open to the public. Ludwigshafen was rebuilt as a modern city and this is best illustrated to visitors by the Wilhelm-Hack-Museum of modern and contemporary art, which has work by Roy Lichtenstein, Andy Warhol, Kandinsky and Mondrian. A lovely place to experience river life is Rhein Galerie, a world of restaurants and shops on the site of the Zollhof harbour.

Next comes Speyer, where its UNESCO-listed cathedral is the jewel of this handsome city, which sits on the flat with peaks rising in the distance. The Romanesque basilica was founded by Emperor Conrad II in 1030 and eight rulers from the Holy Roman Empire are entombed there. The Cathedral of St Mary and St Stephen was intended to be the biggest in the world when work began in 1030 and it is still the world's largest surviving Romanesque church. Climb the tower of the western city gate, which was started in 1230 and added to right up until the 18th century, for views of the river snaking away. Speyer has several other churches worth visiting but its Jewish heritage is also significant. The ruin of the oldest Middle Ages synagogue still standing can be visited, as well as a Jewish ritual bath – or *mikvah* – dating back to at least 1126.

The Rhine now runs through a fairly flat valley, with a variety of lakes, tributaries and woodland. It's a pleasant journey, with the river forming the border between Germany and France.

The first city in France is Strasbourg, which was swapped between France and Germany several times thanks to wars dating back to the 17th century. Even now, many older people speak Alsatian, the Germanic dialect of north-east France. Strasbourg presents a very Germanic version of France, with visitors drawn to the half-timbered buildings of the pretty houses in Quai de la Petite France, once home to the city's fishermen and tanners. The tall

Left: The picturesque delights of Strasbourg on one of the many tiny channels the Rhine forms as it passes through the city

houses, festooned with red geraniums in summer, are in the main historic quarter on the Grande Ile, an island between channels of the River Ill – a tributary of the Rhine – which were used to power mills in the Middle Ages. Now UNESCO-listed, Petite France is a lovely area for walking through a maze of narrow streets past chocolate-box buildings or taking a boat ride past the locks, weirs and bridges of the area including the Barrage Vauban, a fortified dam that provides lovely views of Strasbourg.

The city's other major attraction is the Notre-Dame Cathedral. The red sandstone building took so long to build that it started out as Romanesque in the 12th century, has a 13th-century façade and was completed with a late-Gothic flourish in the 15th century. Climb to the top of the 465ft (142m) spire to see the Rhine at its best. Also visit the 18th-century Palais des Rohan, once residence of the region's bishop-princes and now housing the Museum of Fine Arts and Museum of Decorative Arts.

There's also an Archaeological Museum, reflecting Strasbourg's Roman history and importance during the Middle Ages. Possibly the most modern building of interest, though, is the glass and steel Louise Weiss building housing the European Parliament. Strasbourg is also famed for its Christmas markets on multiple sites; they're typically German with a French twist – you'll find foie gras for sale among the gingerbread hearts.

Among the smaller pretty stops along the Rhine is Breisach, on the German side of the Rhine, where St Stephan's Cathedral looks down on the old town. It's worth walking up the hill to see its mix of Romanesque and Gothic architecture. The view across to the Black Forest is also worth seeing. Breisach is a gateway to the forest and you can get a train from here to Titisee, where you can swim in the picturesque lake and hike through the woods. Most cruise ship companies arrange excursions into the Black Forest to see workshops that still produce the region's distinctive cuckoo clocks, made by traditional methods from local timber, and there are also wine tasting tours.

The final section of river on the journey to Basel is fairly serene, the scenery low-lying though with the hint of the Alps ever present in the distance. Although it is

Switzerland's second largest city the old town is mostly quite peaceful. Basel straddles the river but the older quarter is on the left bank, which is higher with lovely views back down to the water from Basel Minister, where the humanist, Erasmus, is buried. The controversial 15th-century Dutch scholar was attracted to the university at Basel and the city is now reaping the rewards of that cultural heritage.

There's an entrancing old town of cobbled streets that rises from the river up to the minster, with the medieval-looking Rathaus – city hall – a colourful building of romantic towers and courtyards with a 17th-century trompe

Above: The elegant stone Middle Bridge in the medieval city of Basel sits on the site of one of the very first Rhine crossings

l'oeil by the artist Hans Block decorating the façade. This is still the city's council chamber, although you can take a tour of the inside, and it's right next to the market square, which has stalls every day of the week. There are three city gates dating back to the 1400s and much of the old town has picturesque 15th-century buildings.

But Basel also has good modern architecture, including Kunstmuseum Basel and its three art gallery venues. This has works by Hans Holbein, Picasso, Monet, Gauguin and Cezanne, plus other internationally renowned artists. Nearby is Tinguely Fountain from the 1970s, a set of humorous water-spouting sculptures by Jean Tinguely that somehow sums up the best of the old and new that can be seen along the Rhine today.

The river past Basel is not navigable for larger cruise ships. But from the Schifflände dock there are several-hour cruises to the town of Rheinfelden, which can be combined with a train ride back. Or you can simply sample the river on one of the four tiny ferries that travel between Basel's five bridges using only the power of the current.

71

THE RHÔNE AND THE SAÔNE

Head for the Med, with a decent glass of wine

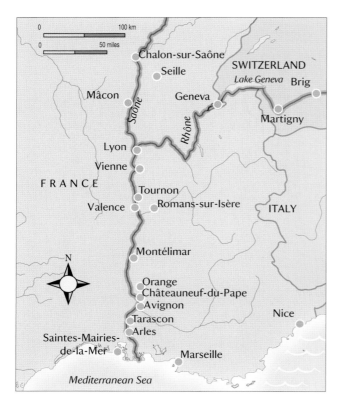

Right: Lavender, a sight that fills the south, against the remains of Avignon's famed bridge, officially known as Pont Saint-Bénézet

The Rhône and Saône go together like wine and cheese, two rivers that combine mountains and sun in the southeast of France. The former is the star, the latter playing a supporting role joining halfway through. It's a combination that makes for a glorious river cruise.

The Rhône starts as run-off from the Rhône Glacier, more than 7,000ft (2,100m) up in the Valais, in the Swiss Alps, at first a raging mountain stream then as a powerful river. It's a journey of 500 miles (800km) from the ice to the warm Mediterranean. Passing through the towns of Brig and Martigny, it then flows into Lake Leman (Lake Geneva). Leaving the lake it's then into France and west to

Right: The single tower of the Passerelle du Palais-de-Justice bridge in Lyon, the city where many cruises start

Opposite: The city of Vienne, just to the south of Lyon, a place that is packed with exceptional Roman remains to visit

the city of Lyon, where the Saône comes in, from the north. It's only around here that the Rhône becomes seriously navigable.

The Saône, a much gentler river, has come 300 miles (480km) from France's Vosges region. Used as a water highway since Greek and Roman times, steamboat services started in Lyon in the early 19th century and ran south to the Roman city of Arles until the mid 20th century. The river runs due south, joined at one point by the Isère (pouring in from the Alps after passing through the city of Grenoble and, earlier, through the chic ski resort of Val d'Isère) just before the town of Valence.

The river often splits into two channels, such as when it passes through the city of Montélimar, and, again, at Avignon with the remains of its famed bridge jutting out from the shore. The River Durance arrives from the east and 25 miles (40km) later you're in Arles. At the city you enter the wild, flat Camargue, a protected landscape, and the same distance again gets you to the warmth of the Mediterranean, although where the sea starts and the river ends is difficult to discern.

The Rhône has a magic that's found nowhere else, where the soft purple hue of lavender fields and the picturesque march of some of France's leading vineyards coat the rolling landscape that's also filled with Roman relics. It's somewhere that can truly be appreciated from contemporary river cruise ships, many of which have fold-back glass walls so that an entire cabin can be a sun-filled balcony, and all of which have expansive sun decks.

This is the land of Beaujolais, Burgundy and Mâcon wines; cruises, which tend to take in both rivers, often major on the wine route. A regular starting point is the town of Chalon-sur-Saône in the Beaujolais region. It's on the Saône maybe 50 miles (80km) north of the wine hub of Mâcon and the same again from Lyon.

Lyon is one of those often overlooked cities, one that rarely conjures up any images in people's minds, yet it is the gateway to both the Alps and wine country, a gastronomic delight, a place filled with medieval and Renaissance architecture, and two rivers, as the Rhône and Saône don't merge until they've passed through its heart.

Heading south from Lyon, its cathedral standing guard, the Rhône passes parks and docks. There's a 10-mile (16km) stretch of canal that runs parallel to the main, albeit narrow, river, wedged up against the A7 road to the south coast. After this the river widens as hills rise up around it. First call is Vienne, a major Roman settlement with plenty of sights – the Temple of Augustus and an open-air theatre – as well as fortifications from other eras on the hills that circle the town.

It's a bucolic landscape as you head south, the river wide and mellow amid a green, rolling backdrop. At little

Saint-Pierre-de-Bœuf (where the Île de la Platière nature reserve sits between the river and the tiny offshoot) another canal section breaks away for a few miles.

The next major town is Tournon, where the river weaves though a wide valley floor. Château de Tournon, a 16th-century castle, filled with relics and art, much related to the Rhône, sits against a rocky backdrop overlooking the river. Just south of here the River Isère arrives and the scenery gets craggier, the mountains of the Ardèche rising to the west. The Parc de l'Epervière is on the riverbank in the town of Valence on the east side, a lovely place to walk with views of the peaks and medieval Castle Crussol.

The riverbanks are increasingly busy, with towns such as Montélimar, as well as plenty of villages. A little further on is the holy grail of wine areas as the hilltop village of Châteauneuf-du-Pape rises up. A medieval castle, built in the 14th century for Pope John XXII, sits on top and dominates the skyline. Everywhere you look the flat surrounding land is planted with vines and signs advertising tastings at the various estates sit alongside every road.

Avignon is nearing and the river splits in two, creating a several-mile-long island of farmland. In the city it's on the eastern channel, when the island has reduced to a city-centre sliver, that the Pont d'Avignon sits, its four 12th-century stone arches a bridge to nowhere but one on which to stand to appreciate the river. Avignon is a living museum with rich Roman artefacts and plenty more from down the centuries, not least the Palais des Papes, the papal palace that is one of the biggest medieval Gothic buildings in Europe, dazzling in its sheer scope.

The river has divided into two again when it arrives at the towns of Beaucaire on the west side and, across bridges that leap both channels and a narrow, tree-covered island, Tarascon. The latter is a calm little place, cabin cruisers tethered to the banks where the large, modern cruise vessels also moor.

Some cruises head farther south than Tarascon for a round-trip into the Carmargue. These give a chance to visit Saintes-Maries-de-la-Mer, the region's tiny capital, several miles west of the river's mouth. The Petit Rhône, which leaves the main river just above Arles, forms much of the western boundary of the national park and runs along the edge of what is little more than a village. There's a fabulous beach, lagoons and walks through the Ornithological Park of Pont de Gau with its huge population of birds that includes the wonderful pink flamingos that enjoy this part of the world.

There's plenty more boating to be done around here – fishing and sightseeing trips from Martigues just to the east and excursions from the ancient harbour of Marseilles only 30 miles (48km) away.

I'LL DRINK TO THAT...

The Saône is often offered for a wine cruise, sometimes made as a round trip from Lyon. Chalon-Sur-Saône, the northernmost point of travel, is only 10 miles (16km) south of Beaune, the heart of the Burgundy region and ripe for an excursion. With the rolling, sun-drenched Côte d'Or vineyards all around, the town with its cobbled streets is famed for an annual wine auction at the Hôtel-Dieu, a 15th-century former hospital, and cruise tastings are often held here.

At Mâcon, visitors go ashore for a tour of the Beaujolais Wine Route, passing by the top-notch Pouilly-Fuissé vineyards and the Roche de Solutré, a limestone rock that juts out from the top of a hill and can be seen for miles. Hameau Duboeuf, not far from the river just south of Mâcon, is a theme park-like attraction devoted to the history of winemaking at the Vins Georges Duboeuf estate.

When not visiting, the sleek modern cruise ships are a delight on which to sit back and gaze at the wine country that you're passing through. But there is plenty to do. From little Belleville there are usually tours to Beaujeu,

capital of the Beaujolais region, a little town strung out along a low, vineyard-covered valley but with wine and good food aplenty.

Yet while some cruises stick to the Saône, for the most part this stretch of river is combined with the Rhône for a trip to the very edge of the Med.

Opposite: The perfect vision of the South of France as the Rhône flows through Tournon, near where the River Isère arrives

Above: Cruise ship *Emerald Sky* passes the remains of the fabled bridge at Avignon on its voyage to the sun

THE SAVA
Central European delights without ever reaching the sea

The Sava is one of the longest rivers in Europe. It flows for a little more than 600 miles (960km) from the mountains of Slovenia until it reaches the Danube, one of the continent's few major rivers not to flow directly into the sea. This region, south of the Alps, is a place that toys with Mediterranean warmth from spring until late in the year with serious heat in the heart of summer, particularly as you head south, giving it a languid charm.

The Sava first appears as the Nadiža waterfall on a rocky cliff face then runs underground until rising as a lake in Zelenci nature reserve near the ski resort of Kranjska Gora, close to the point where Slovenia, Austria and Italy meet. The river cuts through both the Slovenian capital, Ljubljana, and the Croatian capital, Zagreb, yet is shallow and marshy offering river traffic little scope. There's a 210-mile (336km) stretch along the length of the Croatia and Bosnia-Herzegovina border, that flows through a flat landscape with no major cities, although bridges link towns on either bank – the Croatian town of Sisak is as far as most river traffic can get.

The river wanders through Serbia, much of it surrounded by swampy ground and forest, often nature reserves. It reaches the Danube 725 miles (1,160km) from the Black Sea. At the confluence the Sava splits briefly in two as it rounds Great War Island, the right-hand fork also passing Kalemegdanska Terrace, a park encompassing Belgrade Fortress, and only a stroll from the shops and hip bars.

River cruises here aren't widely available but major companies do operate. Cruises run between Belgrade and Sisak (some combine this stretch with the Danube up to Budapest).

Voyages cross the plain of Vojvodina, Serbia's agricultural heartland, visiting places such as Iriski Venac, surrounded by monasteries, a beguiling mix of Byzantine and Baroque in style. Brčko, sitting behind tree-lined riverbanks in Bosnia, was torn apart by the troubles in the 1990s but is still an intriguing mix of Austro-Hungarian styles with Ottoman influences thrown in.

Slavonski Brod, a modest Croatian city, developed as an important river crossing. Well-preserved Brod Fortress is a

Baroque reminder of the Austro-Hungarian Empire's attempts to keep the Ottoman Empire, across the water, at bay. There's a lovely promenade on the now-peaceful river, along what was once the frontier of two powerful entities. Before reaching Sisak, and near the regular call of Jasenovac, is vast Lonjsko Polje, a protected wetland that follows the curves of the river. This a place where the white stork rules, both at the riverbank and in the picture-postcard villages. Čigoč, just before reaching Sisak (on one of the many ox-bow lakes that line the Sava), was even named Europe's first European Stork Village due to the proliferation of nests on the roofs of its picturesque

wooden houses. The scenery is languid and the edges of the river are often cloaked first with water lilies, then with banks of reeds.

The river all but twirls through the town of Sisak, venturing north as the River Kupa joins from the west. Wedged between the two is the old town, its 16th-century fortress (now a museum) the perfect place to learn about the river and its people.

THE SEINE

From Paris to the North Sea

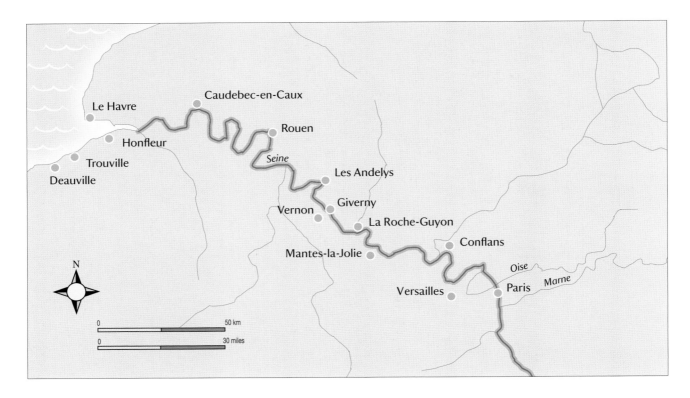

Standing on the side of the Seine, the Eiffel Tower looming in the warmth of the clear blue sky, Paris is a delight. One can't help but love the cosmopolitan feel of France's greatest river; the artists and the musicians who make the grand riverbank walks so vibrant. Standing on the deck of a riverboat after the sun's gone down as the tower erupts into its nightly lightshow, then slowly setting off on a journey all the way to the sea makes it all the more exciting. Yet it's from Paris that it catches the imagination, a journey past châteaux and fortresses, vineyards and farms, French history in all its glory. The Eiffel Tower eventually disappears behind other buildings as the river starts a series of hairpin loops as it heads through the suburbs.

The Seine flows 480 miles (770km) from the woods at the village of Source-Seine near Dijon in the east all the way to the English Channel between the resort town of Le Havre on the north bank and the medieval fishing port of

Right: One of river cruising's greatest sights is sailing through the heart of Paris with the Eiffel Tower as a backdrop

Honfleur on the south. It's already gone more than half its distance by the time it reaches Paris, most of that accessible to small pleasure craft and some of it open to smaller cruise boats.

Poissy is home to a vast Peugeot car factory yet, sitting on the inside of a bend with grassy banks and the remains of an ancient stone bridge, you could, if you look in the right direction, be in the heart of the countryside. From here the river encounters a few hills with great limestone bluffs appearing on the left. Stretches of picturesque holiday cabins and bungalows appear as the river continually widens then narrows, curving and meandering. By the time you reach Mantes-la-Jolie you're really in the countryside

and the grand Gothic church of Notre-Dame looks far too big for its setting.

While much of the town is unremarkable, the stone bridge and the river setting – the Seine split in two by a long, rural island – was painted by Manet, Monet and Renoir during the Impressionist explosion, while the bridge found itself with new fame in 1944 by being the first Seine crossing liberated by the Allies.

On the north bank the Seine now starts following Vexin Français Natural Regional Park, a vast area of forests, hills and pretty villages. Up around the next bend is the village of La Roche-Guyon. It's dominated by the monumental, medieval castle-like 12th-century Château de La Roche-Guyon cut into a chalk cliff topped with a forbidding tower. It is particularly evocative when lit at night and opened to intimate classical concerts for cruise passengers.

It's only 15 miles (24km) to perhaps the most famous stop, the town of Vernon. Nearby (not far from the river) is Giverny, a village known for the house and gardens of Claude Monet. Ten years after he moved here in 1883, he managed to get the gurgling Les Mayeux river, a Seine tributary, diverted at Epte to serve his Oriental-themed retreat (surrounded by tree-high bamboo) and form a lake filled with iconic water lilies. First impressions might be that this is busier than the heart of Paris yet one can't but love the gardens (flowers are changed regularly so there's always something to see) and brightly painted cottage.

From here it's simple, relaxed countryside for a while until the river rounds a bend to the right, a large lake filling the bend behind the trees. A chalk ridge then rises up on the same side, pinning the road to the riverbank. Sitting on

Above left: Château de La Roche-Guyon is often the setting for classical music recitals for cruise passengers

Left: The lily ponds, recorded in so many paintings by Claude Monet, amid the fabulous gardens at his house at Giverny

the ridge is the imposing sight of Château Gaillard, Richard the Lionheart's stronghold built in the final years of the 12th century to protect the nearby city of Rouen from attack. The château is massive. Much of the original was broken up; only one of the five towers survives but it's still an awe-inspiring sight. Cruises call here, at the village of Les Andelys, and a walk up the hill is a way to experience glorious views of the river snaking away.

As the river flows onwards, the chalk ridge shelters delightful riverside houses, some grand, some petite, but finally comes down to earth as the Seine swings left and Rouen opens up on both banks. The city is a game of two halves, and not dependent on which side of the river you

Below: Château Gaillard, fortress of Richard the Lionheart, looms over the Seine and its limestone cliffs at the village of Les Andelys

are on. You arrive in a demure river city that divides to pass placid Ile Lacroix with its parks and apartment blocks, river cruise ships settling on the northern bank. And you leave a serious working port that's just around the bend. It's not that river cruises can't head any farther but there are far bigger ships, including ocean cruise ships.

Rouen Cathedral is one of the great sights of the Seine, three-mismatched Gothic towers, the middle one topped incongruously with a 19th-century cast iron spire (giving it the kudos of, for several years, being the world's tallest building). Claude Monet, when he wasn't gardening, painted the cathedral a number of times. But the city has more; it's where Joan of Arc was burned at the stake and the modernist church at the spot is a glorious contrast to the cathedral. Rouen is also a lovely place for riverside city

walks – and a hard place to leave, but there's plenty to look forward to.

After Rouen, the Seine makes an almighty sweep at first past and then through the wilds of the Roumare National Forest, a place of majestic stands of trees and grand walks, the prospect of wild boar or deer with mighty antlers popping up. The greenery gives way to Des Boucles de la Seine Normande nature park, a more laid-back taste of Normandy, with white-washed cottages and timber-framed buildings.

A regular cruise ship call is Caudebec-en-Caux, a town with a neat promenade lined with shops and bars. There's also MuséoSeine, a history of the river in Normandy in a modern boathouse setting; there are real boats amongst contemporary exhibits on towns, fishing and more. From

here to the sea is a charming cruise through France, passing Villequier, backed by more limestone cliffs, and the old
port of Saint-Aubin-sur-Quillebeuf (with its little cross-
river car ferry), cruising under Tancarville suspension
bridge and coming up on the sky-reaching Pont de
Normandie suspension bridge crossing what by now is the
open water of an estuary.

Now, on the left is Honfleur, not that you'd really know it.
The quayside is simple and bare with the town and its
ancient port down a short waterway ending in Bassin
Carnot. The stone quaysides here are what history is about,
yachts and fishing boats bobbing, half-timbered buildings
housing restaurants and bars – most selling fish and shellfish – that spill out on to the pavement, and market stalls
selling fresh sea salt, bottles of Calvados…and more
shellfish.

It's a very different place and a very different atmosphere from the Seine in the heart of trendy Paris yet this is
what the river is all about, a journey through the ages and
through the wonders of France.

Opposite: Rouen's magnificent cathedral, a favourite subject of Claude Monet, is a stirring sight as you arrive on the Seine

Above: Bassin Carnot, part of the ancient port of the medieval town of Honfleur, where the Seine meets the North Sea

THE BIG SHIPS

The Seine isn't simply there for a river cruise, it's a river
that makes for an impressive ocean cruise. Medium-sized
cruise ships can make it all the way to Rouen. The wide
open waters of the estuary between Le Havre and Honfleur
feel like the sea and ocean ships often visit one or both.

The former, all but obliterated in the Second World War,
is a surprisingly engaging town, much of it rebuilt in understated modernist style and all of it within walking distance
of the port. It's not a place that can be visited by river craft,
effectively out on the ocean, while Honfleur, tucked away
on the riverbank, can take both. There's something exciting about being in a big ship on a river and here you'll find
yourself gazing down at villages, at country houses and at
much smaller craft as you sedately move along a waterway
that at times seems much too small.

THE SHANNON
Water, whiskey and a whole lot more

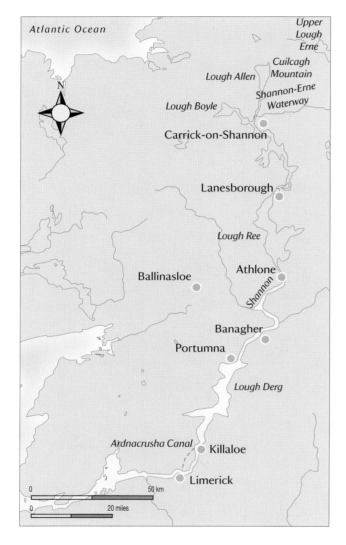

Right: Cabin cruisers, a regular sight on much of the Shannon, are still for the night on the placid setting of Lough Ree

Below right: The remains of the 1,500-year-old monastery at Clonmacnoise stand on a hillside gazing over the Shannon

sometimes narrow, involving stretches of canal. Rarely is it deep, so river journeys here are restricted to small barge cruises, plus self-drive barges and family cruisers.

At the heart of the river is Carrick-on-Shannon, a lovely town. Boat hire is available and from here there are varied experiences. Head north-east on the Shannon-Erne Waterway, 40 miles (64km) long and with 16 locks, which is the canalised River Grainne, opened in 1994. This connects with the River Erne and its two major lakes, Upper and Lower Lough Erne, which offer fishing, nearby pubs and unspoilt countryside.

Carrick itself boasts more than 40 lakes within six miles (10km), either north on the river's spur to Lough Allen, on the Shannon-Erne, or south on the main stretch of river.

Heading south is a more typical river experience, albeit passing through small lakes, until it reaches Lough Ree, 18 miles (26km) long. There are said to be 365 islands here with Inchcleraun the site of a monastery, including the remains of several churches, and Hodson's Pillar isle laying claim to be the geographical centre of Ireland.

Barges can't cross the lake but smaller cruisers can continue down, amid unassuming scenery, to Athlone, one of the river's biggest towns with castle and Kilbeggan Whiskey Distillery (the world's oldest licensed whiskey distillery, from 1757) and beyond. There's the ruined monastery of Clonmacnoise, established 1,500 years ago, with its Romanesque church and round tower, and the town of Shannonbridge, named after the ancient stone bridge with its many arches.

The peat bogs that surround the village are home to an abundance of flora and fauna, and are preserved as a natural habitat for the now rare corncrake. Also lining the river

Ireland's longest river at 225 miles (360km) cuts through this green and pleasant land, dividing east from west with fewer than 30 crossings along the bulk of its length. It rises in the border region of Northern Ireland, but most of its length is in the south where it eventually reaches the Atlantic Ocean at Limerick city on the Shannon Estuary.

It's not Ireland's wildest scenery but it has endless Celtic charm, with rolling fields, castles and grand houses. The river is often wide, opening into lakes (loughs), and

are winding ridges of raised ground (eskers) caused by Ice Age melt. There are marinas with boat hire on this stretch and from Banagher, the Royal Canal and Grand Canal connect to Dublin and the Irish Sea. Portumna, with its castle — actually a semi-fortified 17th-century house — and forest park, has viewing platforms looking over Lough Derg, the biggest lake on the river and second biggest in the country, up to 24 miles (38km) long and eight miles (13km) wide.

Killaloe, at the lake's southern tip, 15 miles (24km) from the coast, is as far as you can go (and some barge cruises reach here from Glasson, at the tip of Lough Ree, near Athlone). Whichever stretch you choose, this is unmistakably Ireland.

THE THAMES

Gentle times on a royal river

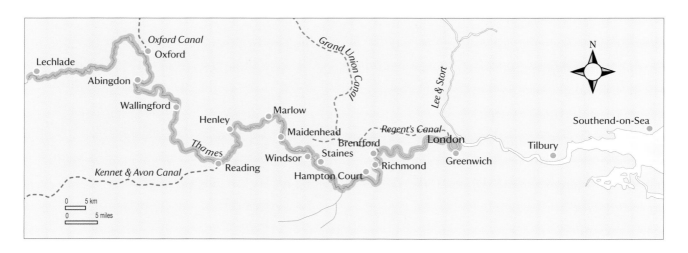

The Thames is truly the heart of England, flowing more than 200 miles (320km) from its source in Gloucestershire across the country and out to the sea on the east coast. And yet, despite its history and its beauty — and its big river attitude as it passes through London — this isn't for main-stream cruising.

The Thames is a timeless river, passing through the university city of Oxford, past the Queen's retreat of Windsor Castle, through chic, upmarket Henley, famed for its annual regatta, and past the grandeur of Henry VIII's country pad, Hampton Court Palace. Teddington Lock, between the towns of Richmond and Kingston to the west of the capital, is the end of the tidal stretch, and prevents anything other than small craft getting farther upriver.

And upriver is tranquil and mostly grassy-banked, as the Thames meanders amongst islands and under low, historic stone bridges. Yet it is possible to experience the river from the water, although you do have to make the effort, through a variety of companies and small, often historic vessels that make you wish you hadn't forgotten your blazer and straw hat.

Salter's Steamers, established in 1858, has a fleet of open boats that ply the Upper Thames between Oxford and the town of Staines. This isn't a single journey, rather a

Below: Turks' historic side-wheeler *Yarmouth Belle*, in operation since 1892, passes under Hampton Court Bridge

series of sightseeing hops, taking in the likes of Windsor, Marlow, Maidenhead and Abingdon, but a genteel way to explore – passing the meadows of Runnymede where in 1215 King John signed the Magna Carta, the first step to modern democracy. Here there is also a memorial to US President John F Kennedy.

Overnight cruises are rare these days but the quirky *African Queen* sails from Mapledurham just west of the city of Reading, heading upstream as far as the market town of Wallingford, a 20-mile (32km) putter, passing alongside the Beale Park animal attraction and through discreet Goring. The ship is a little, red-and-white painted, wooden affair for 14 passengers with wood-panelled cabins and a Cape Malay menu.

Nearer London, Turks is another company with history that operates pretty craft. The *Yarmouth Belle*, a traditional English side-wheeler, is one of two vessels from 1892, while another was one of the 'Little Ships' that rescued troops from Dunkirk in the Second World War. These sail as far upstream as Hampton Court Bridge, for the

Palace, and down as far as Richmond with its elegant river frontage (passing historic spots such as Ham House, bestowed in the early 17th century by James I on his son, Henry Frederick, Prince of Wales, and Twickenham's Eel Pie Island, where acts such as the Rolling Stones, The Who and Rod Stewart performed regularly in the early 60s at the Eel Pie Club).

Just before Ham is Teddington Lock, originally opened in 1811, a gentle, grassy place where the placid waters of the Upper Thames stop and the river becomes tidal – drinkers at riverside pubs in Richmond often have trouble getting in the door due to high tide.

Coming into Richmond gaze up at the exquisite houses atop Richmond Hill, and then get off the boat and take a stroll to the top, to see the riverscape (a government-protected view) that J. M. W. Turner immortalised in his painting *View From Richmond Hill*.

The stretch from Richmond onwards doesn't get the riverboat service but the riverside walk.

As we approach London we get into commuter services. MBNA Thames Clippers sail from Putney in the west to Greenwich and the 02 entertainments arena in the east. The fleet of sleek river buses (with bars and some outside seats) are the way to travel through London on the water, a journey passing mighty (and now redeveloped) Battersea Power Station, the Houses of Parliament, the London Eye big wheel and the theatres of the South Bank, the Tower of London then, after passing under Tower Bridge, the Canary Wharf business district and the classical architecture of Greenwich.

City Cruises, with more conventional boats and open-top decks, sails between Westminster and Greenwich for sightseeing but also has lunch, afternoon tea, dinner and entertainment options (even an Elvis impersonator).

LONDON CALLING

There comes a point on the Thames, by Tower Bridge, where sightseeing vessels and cruise ships meet. Small (and generally luxury) ships can sail under the bridge to dock alongside the museum warship *HMS Belfast*, opposite the Tower of London, for visits and for the occasional cruise departure. Sailing from here gives great views over the Tower, the glass towers of Canary Wharf and Greenwich, with its historic tea clipper *Cutty Sark* and the

Above: To the west of London the Thames quickly becomes a place of grassy banks, idyllic houses and pottering about in small craft

Right: Tower Bridge opens wide to welcome Silversea's luxury cruise ship *Silver Wind* into the very heart of London

grand Royal Naval College. Some ships have also been anchoring at Greenwich, however the new London City Cruise Port just down river will accommodate bigger ships and increase the number of cruises to London.

A little farther, at Royal Victoria Docks (near the northern end of the Emirates Air Line river-crossing cable car) you can get a feel for the Thames in Sunborn London, a permanently docked 420ft luxury yacht turned hotel.

There are also regular cruises from the port of Tilbury, just down river from the Queen Elizabeth II bridge, where P&O liners used to dock in the early 20th century. The terminal, opened in 1930, is all but a museum to the thousands of 'Ten Pound Poms', who set off for a new life in Australia in the post-war years and the early immigrants from the Caribbean. Passengers still board ships via ornate gangways from the early days.

Sadly, from here to the sea, while the river is wide enough for many ships, the landscape is featureless, flat and lacking in places for cruises to call. Only the seaside resort of Southend at the river's mouth stands out, thanks to its pier, at 1.34 miles (2.16km) the world's longest.

THE TISZA

Cut down to size by the will of the people

A river truly in the control of the people. The Tisza flows the length of Hungary (and through much of what used to be Hungary during its grandest days) and had a tendency to flood profusely, so in 1846 the Hungarians took charge in a project lasting more than 30 years.

István Széchenyi was at the helm, one of the country's great politicians and someone with a penchant for waterways – he led improvements to the Danube near the Black Sea and backed the first real bridge between Buda and Pest, the British-built Chain Bridge that even today is a stirring sight for Danube cruise passengers.

The result was that the Tisza's 870-mile (1,400km) length through the country was chopped by creating shortcuts to 600 miles (960km). It is still far from straight yet serves to illustrate how things used to be, endless oxbow lakes and other cast-off pieces of river on either side.

Below: The river makes a big sweep through the city of Szeged, with the twin towers of the Votive Church looming over the rooftops

The Tisza springs up in the Chornohora mountains of Ukraine, hugs Ukraine's border with Romania, darts across the north of Hungary (forming the Hungary-Slovakia border for a couple of miles) before heading south across Hungary, joining the Danube in Serbia. It is, however, the Hungarian stretch across the big open spaces of the plains that beguiles travellers.

Tokaj, a charming town backed by hills in the heart of wine country, is the place for sightseeing boat trips as well as being the starting point for occasional (but big name) river cruises, which head down to the Danube then often on to Budapest.

The Tisza meanders between tree-lined banks that give way to sweeping vineyards interspersed with fields of sunflowers so prevalent in this part of the world. Not too far south amid the farmland, the river forms the edge of two overspill lakes several miles wide; on one the little town of Tiszafüred has lawns that sweep down to the water's edge, on the other is Lake Tisza Beach, a charmingly unhurried spot where people swim and barbecue.

Other stops for cruises and pleasure trips are likely to include Csongrád, a pretty little town with a beach gazing over at the tree-lined bank opposite. Just along from here is a vast area of protected grassland and forest that stretches along the river for miles, a park filled with history – windmill, animals, the museums of Ópusztaszer National Heritage Park – along with lakes, little waterways, and several ox-bow lakes.

At the other side of the greenery is Szeged, the biggest city of the Great Plain and third largest in the country. Its buildings are more modern than in much of Hungary, due to the great flood of 1879 – just before the river works were completed – which swept away all but several hundred houses. Sitting close to the river, the Votive Church with its twin 299ft (91m) towers was part of the new wave, started in 1913 but only finished in 1930 due to the interruption of the First World War.

Szeged Synagogue with its grand dome is regarded as a masterpiece of Magyar style, mixing Art Nouveau, Moorish, Gothic and Roman elements. The city sits on the Hungary-Serbia border (Romania's just up the road) but the Tisza has another 100 miles (160km) to go, flowing through a mix of agriculture and small towns, before reaching the Danube.

THE VOLGA AND THE SVIR
Two rivers, and a journey through time

Above: The monumental statue of Vladimir Lenin towers over the end of the Moscow Canal at the town of Dubna

These two rivers make up one monumental journey through the heart of one of the world's least understood countries. The Volga is the longest river in Europe, flowing 2,300 miles (3,680km) from the Vaidai Hills north-west of Moscow to Astrakhan on the Caspian Sea, near the border with Kazakhstan. The Svir flows a modest 140 miles (235km) westwards from Lake Onega to Lake Ladoga, Europe's two biggest lakes. But, with deft use of various other waterways, the pair combine to link the Soviet grandeur of the capital city, Moscow, and the arts and elegance of St Petersburg.

In between is a landscape that frequently feels as though it hasn't been touched for centuries, a place where Europe touches Asia, with the people who live in these remote parts from a different world. Yet this is a route of luxury cruises operated by major international companies, an adventure through time.

The journey actually begins on the Moscow River in Moscow itself, the banks adorned with impressive buildings, packed with sights such as the Kremlin and Red Square. In the north-west of the city there's the entrance to the Moscow Canal. This 80-mile (128km) waterway, built by slave labour in the 1930s, is the direct link with the Volga, passing through forests and reservoirs. It ends, under the watchful eye of an 82ft (25m) statue of Lenin, at

the town of Dubna (noted for its science institute, not least for its nuclear research) where the Volga opens into the vast Ivankovo Reservoir, several miles wide and some 20 miles (32km) long.

The voyage continues along the Volga itself, heading north-west, through open countryside and the occasional town, passing onion-domed churches and quaint rural hotels. A big attraction is Uglich, one of Moscow's Golden Ring cities where Russia's history is preserved. Sights include the church of St Dmitri-on-the-Blood, on the site where Ivan the Terrible's son, Dimitri, was murdered in 1591. Then comes Yaroslavl, a World Heritage Site and the unofficial capital of the Golden Ring, inundated with churches and with the breathtaking Spaso-Preobrazhensky (Saviour Transfiguration) Monastery.

Above: The heart of Moscow, from where cruises head out through history across the great expanse of Russia to the city of St Petersburg

The river reaches another vast reservoir, the Rybinsk, and the main flow turns east towards the Caspian Sea. From here, though, the Volga-Baltic Waterway heads for the Baltic through mile upon mile of untouched country-side. The mixture of rivers and canals runs something like 230 miles (370km) from the town of Cherepovets, at the far end of the 80-mile (130km) body of water, all the way to Lake Onega.

While it's the Volga-Baltic Waterway, it's not neatly con-structed, starting simply as the River Sheksna. This river is initially a mile wide flowing first to the east, then north,

Above: Ornate onion-domed churches can be found in so many places yet never fail to appeal with their extravagant colours

Right: The fabulous city of St Petersburg is filled with places to see, but don't ignore the wonderful riverside walks

sometimes narrower, sometimes through reservoirs, until it enters Lake Beloye, 35 miles (56km) wide.

The journey north takes in the Vytegra and Kovzha Rivers, both incorporated into the early 19th-century Mariinsk canal system that was upgraded at various times in the mid 20th century by gulag prisoners of the Communists, completed, with modern locks, in 1964. Lake Onega is up to 200 miles (320km) long but the waterway joins at the southern tip and the River Svir exits a mere 20 miles (32km) away.

Cruises, however, make the most of what is Europe's second biggest lake, heading north to the island of Kizhi, a UNESCO World Heritage Site and open-air museum of ancient timber houses, windmills and churches, dominated by the fairytale Preobrazhenskaya (Transfiguration) Church, from 1714, built without a single nail. Sailing along the lake is like being at sea, following the coast. It can get choppy but the huge, flat expanse of water combined with the pancake-flat land and the even huger sky are entrancing.

The Svir runs gently south-west, at first modest in size but occasionally bursting out into lakes, for 140 miles (234km) until it reaches Lake Ladoga. The route is wild and forested, occasional small towns popping up along with heavy industry and the odd dam and locks, heavy barges lumbering their way along. A regular cruise call is the museum-village of Mandrogi with its vodka museum, bath houses and shops.

Lake Ladoga is pretty much 100 miles (160km) wide in any direction, making it the biggest lake in Europe, but the beaches and little boats that line the shores, which themselves are low and a mix of forest and marsh, give it a gentle, friendly touch.

The Svir flows into Lake Ladoga, the Neva flows from there to the sea. Neva Bay on the Gulf of Finland is only 30 miles (48km) away but the Neva River takes a long dip southward, making its way past charmingly rural housing into the heart of St Petersburg. It may be Russia's second biggest city but it has a calm, sophisticated feel, cut through with many canals that get it the name 'Venice of the North'.

The Neva splits into a handful of channels as it cuts through the city and there's plenty to be seen as you walk alongside them – grandiose mansions, parks, little shops. Simply standing on the seafront as the Neva – and a journey halfway across a continent – ends is thrill enough but other sights need to be seen. Catherine Palace, the rococo 18th-century summer residence of the Russian tsars; the vast collection of art in the Hermitage Museum; the St Petersburg Ballet and more. Ocean cruise ships call here as well as the many river ships, so it is a major tourist destination.

This is a voyage that might not be on a single river but which is a fascinating insight to both a country and the tangled web of waterways that make it possible to cover great distances.

DREAM VOYAGE

While Moscow-St Petersburg is the voyage most offered by cruise companies, *Volga Dream* sails 1,865 miles (3,000km) from Moscow to Astrakhan. The experience,

including nights in both cities, takes up to two weeks.

It's a journey through a land that veers from medieval landscapes to modern industry, forests to wide plains. Calls include Uglich and Yaroslavl, then Nizhny Novgorod (known for many years as Gorky), full of ancient sites and once a place of exile for political exiles.

Russian Orthodox churches give way to mosques as the river heads east. First is Kazan, capital of the Republic of Tatarstan, then Samara where the river loops around the low, tree-covered Zhiguli Mountains. The elegant embankment is a place to stroll with the bleakly beautiful steppes stretching away. The river is a mile wide and, at the edge of the city is joined by the Samara and shatters into channels, lakes and wetlands before regaining its composure and heading south again, often five miles (8km) wide.

That ends with the dam at Samara Oblast after which the river is smaller, although still a mile wide. After 70 miles (110km), at Saratov (once Yuri Gagarin's home), it breaks out into islands again. It's 300 miles (480km) to the dam at Volgograd (formerly Stalingrad) in a landscape that's basically flat, with the wetland feel of an estuary even though several hundred miles from the Caspian. It's full of World War Two memorials, particularly 'The Motherland Calls' on the lone hill with views that disappear into the haze.

Astrakhan, where river cruises end, is at the start of the Volga delta, 50 miles (80km) from the sea, where the river splits into smaller and smaller offshoots, although the Volga itself does continue, much diminished, through the wetlands. This is an area rich in sturgeon making it the world's caviar capital and Astrakhan a major fishing port. By the time it hits the Caspian (the world's biggest enclosed body of water, and well below sea level), near Kazakhstan, it's a mere shadow of itself, yet still beautiful as it meanders through a bird-filled nature reserve.

Right: The memorial 'The Motherland Calls' on its hilltop setting in Saratov with the River Volga stretching away into the distance

Classic paddlewheeler American Empress
makes her way along the Columbia River

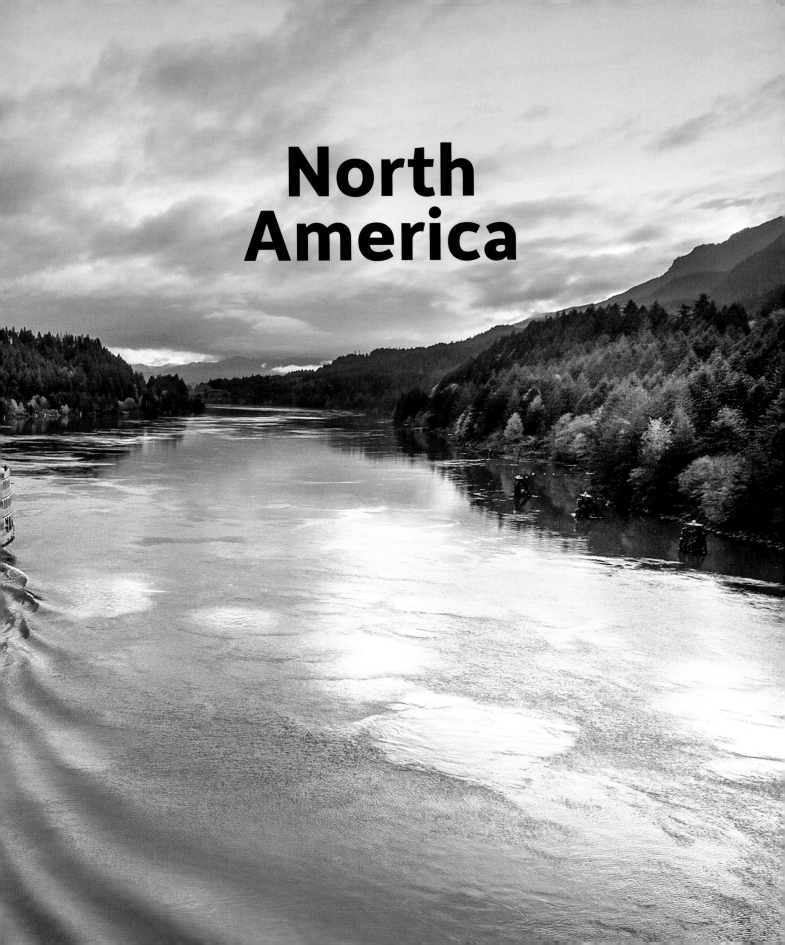

North America

THE COLUMBIA

Cowboys, waterfalls and sea lions

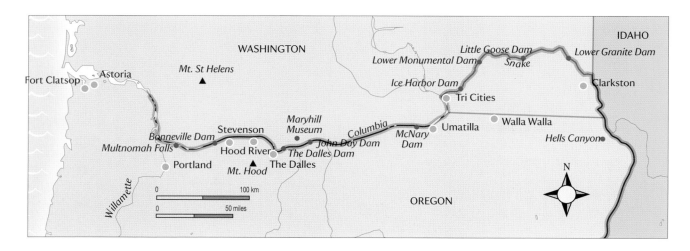

During the night you sail between sandy canyon walls, where you wouldn't be surprised to see the Lone Ranger riding high above, framed by the bright blue sky; the next morning it's a world of mighty temperate rainforest, soaring trees piercing the rain-loaded mist. The Columbia River, in the Pacific Northwest, is a land of giant scenery and giant contrasts.

It rises in the mountains of British Columbia, over the border in Canada and flows first north-west then south, crossing the border into Washington State before turning west and forming the state line between Washington and Oregon all the way to the Pacific, a 1,240-mile (2,000km) journey. It's the latter stretch between Washington State and Oregon that is the most remarkable, much of it through the rugged Columbia Gorge.

Many cruises start on its main tributary, the Snake River that rolls in from the high plains of Idaho. From Clarkston, near Washington's Idaho border, the journey passes through cowboy country yet everything quickly changes, as explorers Captain Meriwether Lewis and Second Lieutenant Willam Clark found more than 200 years ago. Of course in those days there wasn't the McNary Dam, nor John Day Dam, whose lock has a 110ft (33m) drop – the world's tallest until China's Three Gorges project.

Below: *American Empress* heads under Hood River Bridge, with perpetually snow-tipped Mt Hood as a backdrop

Right: The Columbia Gorge opens out with *American Empress*'s brightly-painted paddlewheel shining like a lantern

Above: Multnomah Falls, just across the road that runs alongside the river, thunders constantly as the waters crash down in two stages

First stop is The Dalles (meaning rapids), where Lewis and Clark found their path blocked and took to the river in canoes. The opposite bank is ridged by gnarled peaks, their lush, green, grassy covering looking prehistoric, crying out to be the setting for a sci-fi film.

Prime cruise ship here, with week-long trips, is the modern but traditional-style *American Empress* paddle-wheeler, gaily painted in red and white. Even she looks like a creation from the future in a spot like this. At Columbia Gorge Discovery Centre, timber and stone with windows across the river to more primordial scenery, there are tales of the Columbian mammoth, a creature that reached 13ft (4m), with tusks to match, the biggest mammoth of all.

From here the gorge gets ever mightier. It was created in the last Ice Age when ice blocked a rocky bottleneck creating a lake the size of Montana; when it melted, waters 2,000ft (610m) high swept through.

Sailing through the town of Hood River is one of the most spectacular experiences, the river widening out but the gorge walls creating a wind tunnel and one of the world's leading windsurfing centres. Frail-looking sails fill the choppy waters that manage to remind one of both the Norwegian fjords and England's Lake District. In the distance looms 11,000-ft (3,400-m) Mt Hood, a perpetually snow-tipped volcano.

Next is tiny Stevenson. The ship docks against a wall of pines that climb up a wild mountainside. A salmon jumps from the water and plops back in. A slow-moving Santa Fe freight train trundles past along its riverbank track for what seems like forever, well over 200 cars. Nearby is the giant Bonneville Dam, open for visitors to be mesmerised by a glass-fronted fish ladder, an engineering marvel through which salmon struggle upstream to spawn.

The final stretch of the gorge is fringed by the Old Scenic Highway, built in 1913, another engineering marvel, that twists and turns up to 733ft (225m) Crown Point where Art Deco Vista House, one of America's earliest roadside rest-stops, lords it over the river. Nearby are a string of waterfalls, the king of which is Multnomah Falls, Oregon's highest at 611ft (186m), crashing down just across the road from the riverbank.

The gorge ends as suddenly as it began and the river relaxes into an area of mellow fruitfulness, passing the flood-plain habitat of Steigerwald Lake National Wildlife Refuge with its Red-tailed Hawks and Turkey Vultures, possibly even a Bald Eagle.

Soon the scenery becomes urban as the river enters Oregon's biggest city, Portland, or what seems to be Portland as the city is actually on the south bank with the Washington State suburb of Vancouver (not THE Vancouver) on the north. The Victorian cityscape is entrancing as you pass serenely under rail and road bridges, past wharfs and moored ships, and past the green wilderness of Government Island with its beaches and Great Blue Heron colony.

From here it's 60 miles (95km) to the Pacific. The scenery becomes wild as soon as the city is left behind, passing Ridgefield National Wildlife Refuge, wetlands and forest, a stop-off for many migratory birds as well as deer and even river otters. Other wildlife refuges follow as the river twists across wide-open plains backed by misty mountains. It widens to an estuary dotted with islands where the main town is Astoria on the Oregon bank, five miles (8km) from the sea. This was the end of the trail for Lewis and Clark, and the wide-open setting, alive with its big colony of sea lions, pays homage to the explorers. Fort Clatsop National Memorial, just outside town on the tributary Lewis and Clark River, marks the place where the men and their team spent the 1805-06 winter.

Astoria's four-mile (7km) riverfront walkway is a stroll through time, with historic canneries, cafés, working docks and trendy brewpubs, all beneath the looming cantilevers of the four-mile (7km) Astoria–Megler Bridge on which iconic Highway 101 leaps the river.

For views out to the windblown Pacific, across town and the Coastal Range, and way back along the river's path, climb the 164 steps of Astoria Column. Built in 1926 and modelled on Roman architecture, with a hand-painted frieze, it's a monumental tribute to a monumental river.

Below left: Bald Eagles can often be spotted as they glide above the dense forests that line the banks of the Columbia

Below: Roman-styled Astoria Column, high on a hill, overlooks the spot where the Columbia pours into the Pacific Ocean

THE HUDSON

Where mountains give way to the skyscrapers of New York

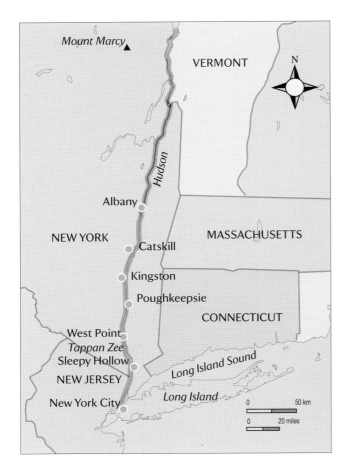

New York's Empire State Building pierces the blue skies as you gaze up from the Hudson. The Rockefeller tower is behind you and the new World Trade Center is closing in fast in what is perhaps the most dramatic end to any river journey.

The Hudson has wended its way 315 miles (505km) from a mountainous wilderness to reach the Atlantic Ocean at New York. It drops 4,300ft (1,300m), mostly in the first 160 miles (256km), the Upper Hudson, down to the dam and locks, dating back to 1916, at Troy, where the river becomes tidal, just north of the state capital, Albany.

The river runs almost directly south through wild yet often delicate New England scenery from its source in the Adirondacks — Lake Tear of the Clouds on New York's highest peak, Mount Marcy. The final stretch, just before it forms the county line between New York and New Jersey, is where the river comes into its own, as Hudson fjord, a wide, glacier-formed stretch with waters up to 175ft (50m) deep in places.

Cruises take place between Albany and New York (often round trips from Manhattan). From Albany the first stop (just after passing the Victorian-era Hudson-Athens lighthouse perched on its mid-river rock) is often Catskill, with the backdrop of the Catskill Mountains, where Clermont State Historic Site was the home of Robert Livingston Junior, the politician who negotiated the Louisiana

Left: Kaaterskill Falls in the hamlet of Haines Falls, on Kaaterskill Creek, which joins the Hudson at Catskill Heights

Below: Hudson-Athens lighthouse, near Catskill, dates from 1874. It's now an historic site and can be visited on boat tours

Purchase and helped draft the Declaration of Independence.

Next stop, Kingston, is home of the riverfront Hudson River Maritime Museum, with the 1898 Steam Tug *Mathilda* in dry dock outside and with its own public moorings. It is one of the places where the river, wide and lake-like, opens up to beaches, where families paddle and swim in the shallows. The placid setting also sees mansions with lawns pouring down to the river. And Rondout Creek splashes down from the Catskills to join the Hudson. At this point Rondout Lighthouse, built in 1915 and accessible only by boat, sits like a riverborne mansion.

Given how close this is to New York, the number of smart houses here is not surprising. Hyde Park has grand river views from the hills that line the banks and the likes of the Astors and Vanderbilts had weekend getaways around here. It's also the birthplace of President Franklin D. Roosevelt and his Springwood estate, now the Franklin D. Roosevelt National Historic Site, is an excursion on most cruise tours. West Point is the home of the famed United States Military Academy with museum and fabulous views over the Hudson Valley. Cruises invariably have tours to visit the academy. The trim, tidy surroundings are a stark contrast to the wilderness of Black Rock Forest Consortium and, farther along, Bear Mountain State Park.

The town of Sleepy Hollow was immortalised in author Washington Irving's *Rip Van Winkle* – his home, Sunnyside, is a National Historic Landmark. Here too is Kykuit, the Rockefeller estate. At Poughkeepsie the Walkway over the Hudson is a restored 1889 railroad crossing, while Mid-Hudson Bridge is a soaring suspension affair.

Hudson Highlands, running between the peaks of Breakneck Ridge and Storm King is where the river starts to become truly dramatic, with panoramas that could come straight from Norway. As it heads south it relaxes into Haverstraw Bay, almost four miles (7km) across, the

widest spot on the estuary. The Bay and Tappan Zee, the body of water to the south, are shallow and salt water starts to take over, with crabs being found near the banks. The striking New Tappan Zee Bridge, its cables strung from modernistic towers, opened in late 2017, spanning the river's second widest point, just north of Sleepy Hollow. The scenery is a picture throughout the summer but later in the year it is spectacular in Fall Foliage mode, a sea of orange and gold that stretches as far as the eye can see.

For much of the way from Haverstraw Bay to New York City the western bank is lined with the Palisades, dramatic cliffs emerging from the trees, then topped with an even layer of foliage, a protected landscape. The George Washington Bridge leaps the river after which the Palisades subside and the towers of Manhattan rise, the Hudson wide and sea-like, the city like an ocean port.

Cruises end in the southern reaches of Manhattan but there's a little farther to go yet. This is the Upper Bay and you don't reach the ocean until you've sailed under the soaring Verrazano-Narrows Bridge into the Lower Bay. To see this part of the river fully it's possible to take a boat trip to Liberty Island, where the Statue of Liberty stands tall, or to Ellis Island nearby where immigrants landed on their way into the US. Or take in the view from a budget trip on a Staten Island Ferry. Many sightseeing cruises from Lower Manhattan have views of Verrazano-Narrows Bridge, the world's longest suspension bridge until pipped by England's Humber Bridge. To see it properly, come from the other direction – cruise ships sail under here (big ones only making it by a matter of feet) and into the Upper bay, docking in East River, the other side of Manhattan.

It's a spectacular place to be whether you're finishing a cruise or getting ready to set sail.

Below: The Statue of Liberty marks the end of the Hudson. There are lots of sightseeing trips on offer from beneath Manhattan's skyscrapers

THE ILLINOIS
Sailing in the lee of Abraham Lincoln

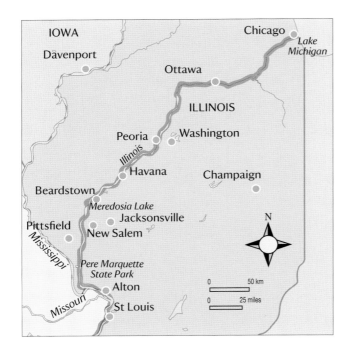

While the Mississippi might be the river that sweeps across the US and through most people's thoughts, the Illinois could be said to be at the heart of the country's constitution.

The river is a tributary of the Mississippi, but a major one, connecting (thanks to the Illinois Waterway canal) Lake Michigan and Chicago in the north-east, on the Canadian border, with the muddy Mississippi near St Louis on the opposite bank, in Missouri. It's a journey or around 270 miles (435km) from its source, just south-east of the lake.

It is a major transport link between the Great Lakes and the Gulf of Mexico but, more importantly, this is Abraham Lincoln's river. The president lived in Illinois, studied to be a lawyer here – and it was along the river that were sowed the seeds of him becoming the most famous of US presidents.

The river has never been a major cruise setting although the launch in 2017 of boutique paddlewheeler *American Duchess* (with its ornate Lincoln Library) is changing that.

The *Duchess* journeys between St Louis, beneath the soaring stainless steel Gateway Arch, and Ottawa – no, not in Canada, but a town a few miles from Chicago.

The scenery is simple and subdued, embodying the spirit of the Midwest, with rich farmland and plains, and an old-time America feel. Before reaching the Illinois there's a short stretch of the Mississippi to negotiate.

Little Alton, in Illinois but still on the Mississippi and surrounded by limestone bluffs, is where the last of the Great Debates of 1858 took place. It was the seventh time that Republican Lincoln met Democratic candidate Stephen Douglas to battle it out for the Illinois place on the US Senate. Lincoln lost but his speeches were published as a book – which was so popular he was nominated for (and won) the 1860 presidential election.

Lincoln had earlier lived in New Salem, between the later state capitol, Springfield, and the Illinois, on the Sangamon River, a tributary of the Illinois. This was 40 miles (65km) from Illinois as the crow flies, much longer by the looping river. Lincoln, a surveyor, studied law in his spare time and by 1835 was practising in Springfield. His tomb is at the city's Oak Ridge Cemetery while the Abraham Lincoln Presidential Library and Museum traces his life.

Yet there's much more in this part of the world than politics. As soon as you're on the Illinois the river becomes a welter of channels, passing the wilds of Pere Marquette State Park. Running as straight as any river can, it heads north with only small communities by its side. It flows past Meredosia National Wildlife Refuge with its five-mile (8km) Meredosia Lake that is a vast area of placid wetlands drifting away to prairie, home to dozens of species of waterfowl and wading birds.

The river passes Big Lake (albeit nowhere near as big as Meredosia Lake), splits into various channels (one called Curry Lake) at pretty Beardstown then passes through a landscape of little lakes and meandering waterways for a

Above: *American Duchess*'s sister ship, *American Queen*, passes the limestone bluffs at Alton, near the Illinois-Mississippi meeting

number of miles. Chautauqua National Wildlife Refuge is yet another huge lake with wetlands, followed by Rice Lake State Fish and Wildlife Area, where deer and even Bald Eagles can be seen.

Then comes Peoria, the largest city on the river and the oldest European settlement in the state, settled by the French in 1680. In its heart the river suddenly blossoms into Peoria Lake, a mile wide and several times as long. Just when you think it's over the narrow channel opens on to Upper Peoria Lake, more than 20 miles (32km) long, the river meandering through another half dozen smaller lakes after that.

The city's Block, a collection of museums and attractions, includes the Riverfront Museum with its Illinois River Experience, an aquarium containing native fish alongside exhibits telling the river's history from the Kankakee Torrent 14,000 years ago, a flood caused by the melting of the Wisconsin Glacier. The Starved Rock State Park, 65 miles (100km) north-east along the river, just past the town of La Salle, cut through by canyons and with a wide lake, is still evidence of the icy deluge.

This is almost the end of most river journeys, with Ottawa, at the confluence of the Illinois and Fox River, just coming up. But it's not the end of the Lincoln connection – this was where the first Lincoln-Douglas debate took place. It was also a major stop on the Underground Railroad, the escape route for slaves, a cause close to the heart of abolitionist Lincoln.

This is as far upstream as big ships can make it and as you head towards Chicago the river is a much more commercial operation than the rural route inland. The Illinois becomes the Des Plaines River as the riverbanks become more built up and the river soon finds itself sidelined by (and running alongside) the Chicago Sanitary and Ship Canal, a 30-mile (48km) link to the Chicago River in the city. Heavy barges and other transport are busy on the waterway that carves through downtown in the shadow of glass skyscrapers before emerging on Lake Michigan.

This final stretch of river can be explored on sightseeing trips from various companies that offer architectural, history, dinner and, of course, drinking cruises in the glass canyons of the city.

Below: The soporific scenery near La Salle, close to Starved Rock State Park with its canyons and other glacial features

Right: Chicago has 43 lifting bridges with a mass opening each spring allowing free passage to Lake Michigan

THE MISSISSIPPI

NEW ORLEANS TO MEMPHIS

A journey from the Gulf through the magic of the South

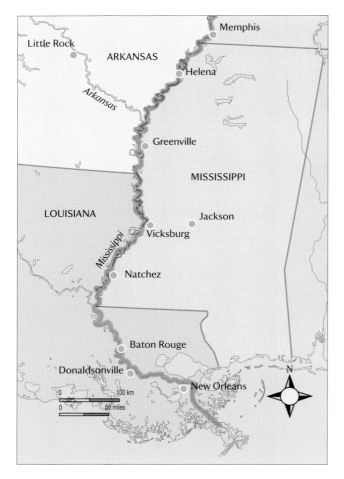

Above: Stanton Hall, just off the Natchez riverfront, was built in 1859 and is now the Carriage House restaurant

New Orleans, a bustling, magical city on the sun-drenched Gulf of Mexico, is the starting point of a cruise that rolls relentlessly through the heart of the American dream. This is where the mighty Mississippi meets the Gulf of Mexico after a 2,320-mile (3,730km) journey from northern Minnesota. Varied stretches serve as cruise itineraries, and each is startlingly different.

The classic stretch of many cruises unites the land of jazz and the land of rock 'n' roll — Memphis. It's a journey on a river often more than a mile (1.6km) wide through the elegant Deep South, passing along the border of Louisiana and Mississippi, then touching Arkansas and into Tennessee. It's a land of cotton fields and sugar cane plantations. *Gone With The Wind*-style mansions will transport you back in time, as will the Civil War battlefields. The Mississippi was a turning point in American history: when Union forces took command of the river, the Civil War was all but over.

Cruises in either direction generally last a week, (although others, lasting several weeks, go all the way to St Paul, Minnesota). Travel is mostly on paddlewheelers, not least the *American Queen*, the largest river steamboat ever built.

Above: The French Quarter of New Orleans is the colourful, music-filled place to start a cruise along the Mississippi

Right: *American Queen*, the world's biggest paddlewheeler, sails through the featureless yet hypnotic scenery of the South

It carries 220 passengers in Victorian splendour but with state-of-the-art facilities, having only been built in 1995.

The Mississippi is tracked by the River Road, a title given to the generally local roads on both banks, as it weaves, sometimes through river plains, often with levees to protect the civilisation that has grown up around it. Flooding is a way of life, with record levels reached in 2011.

Make no mistake, this is a working river, America's water highway, and the 80-mile (130km) stretch from New Orleans to Louisiana's capital, Baton Rouge, is the busiest, thanks to the huge amount of industry alongside. Yet there's beauty too, although small-town America can be hidden behind the relentless raised banks that contain a mighty river that is renowned for its changes in course over thousands of years.

You're barely out of New Orleans when the plantations start. First, and most moving, is Whitney, in the grand style but the only one in Louisiana with a focus on slavery. Next is Laura, followed swiftly by St Joseph, both sugar producers. When it comes to mansions, however, the finest is next door to St Joseph at Oak Alley, a regular cruise call. Running down to the river in Oak Alley Plantation is a

quarter mile of huge live oaks, possibly 300 years old, that form a shady canopy. At the other end is the Greek-style antebellum home, a vision in white with its lofty pillars.

At Rich Bend the river takes a sharp right turn, increasingly passing industrial sites as picturesque cruise vessels mingle with heavy-duty traffic – strings of barges pushed and pulled by tiny tugs. The landscape is flat, the gentle rise of the river bank lined with trees and with fields, rich in flood-plain minerals, stretching away beyond.

The hypnotic spell is broken as you round another bend and see the towering cantilever Sunshine Bridge. When

built in 1964 it was the only bridge across the Mississippi between New Orleans and Baton Rouge. It stretches 8,236ft (2,510m) from side to side – bridges here have to go on seemingly forever to leap not only the wide river but also the swamps and flood plains on either side.

At the hairpin bend of Point Houmas another plantation, Houmas House, is right on the River Road, the mansion peering through the trees. There's barely enough time to straighten up before a swing the other way at forested Bringier Point and Hermitage Plantation.

The pockets of civilisation are reminders that, despite a tree-lined bank so far away, you're not sailing along a country's coastline. Just up on the left is Donaldsonville. Here is waterfront Fort Butler, built where Bayou Lafourche, a major outlet to the Gulf, meets the river. An 1863 Confederate attack was seen off here by former English ship, the gunboat USS *Princess Royal*. Now Donaldsonville's pretty streets feature individual shops and quaint places to pop into for a coffee.

Opposite: Nottaway Plantation stands guard over the Mississippi, the south's biggest antebellum mansion, carefully restored

Above: The statue of forward-thinking, former Louisiana governor, Huey P Long outside the State Capitol, Baton Rouge

The Mississippi weaves onward, passing Nottoway Plantation, the mansion lording it over the river, then Bayou Goula Towhead. The latter is one of the larger of the river's many islands, unoccupied and well over a mile long, a microcosm of Louisiana scenery – with its beaches, jungle-like trees poking out of the swamp and riverbank cypresses distant in either direction.

Next comes little Plaquemine, notable for its Sunshine Ferry puttering across, then the abandoned town of Morrisonville – now little more than a vast chemical plant after contamination meant that the entire population was relocated in the 1990s.

From one of the most unsavoury places on the river it's a short distance to the state capital, Baton Rouge. Passing under lofty Howard Wilkinson Bridge, carrying the I-10

road, the river is home to the destroyer USS *Kidd*, now a museum. Nearby is Louisiana's Old State Capitol, a castle-like building now a museum of state politics. While the right bank is a place of walks and greenery, the opposite side is strictly business with the oil tanks of Port Allen — although with the river half a mile (800m) wide, even here the views aren't a problem. However, a little farther along the city bank turns into a vast ExxonMobil plant, one of the world's biggest petrochemical complexes.

After passing under the city's second crossing, Huey P Long Bridge, the river turns its back on Baton Rouge,

veering sharply west. This is swamp country, Baton Rouge Bayou off to the right, although both banks are swathed in trees. Here comes Profit Island, several miles (5km) long, formed by the gradual drifting together of two smaller islands. Kayakers land on the sandbars while the island itself is a jungle of hardwood trees. Industry drifts away as wilderness takes hold until the looming trees are suddenly dwarfed by the pillars and cables of John James Audubon Bridge, a rare new crossing that, in 2011, replaced a ferry.

Other islands come and go before Shreve's Bar, which has idyllic beaches reminiscent of a Caribbean isle. It's named after Captain Henry Miller Shreve who opened the Mississippi to steamboat navigation. It's here that the river expands to its full mile and a half width and reaches Mississippi, the state line following the channel. The landscape is hillier yet still featureless, characterised by the lack of civilisation, the river being too strong to allow building close by.

Then comes Natchez, a place of southern elegance that has managed to exist on the river's edge since 1716 (it's the oldest city on the Mississippi). Natchez National Historical Park celebrates the city on the pre-Civil War Melrose estate with its visitor centre and Greek Revival mansion along with other properties.

Vicksburg is where the river is at its most picturesque, a grand sweep between high bluffs. The genteel streets and charming buildings give no sign that this was at the heart of American history when, during the Civil War, the city surrendered after the 47-day Siege of Vicksburg, when Union forces gained control of the entire Mississippi. Vicksburg National Military Park – on the itinerary of almost all cruises – commemorates the troops of both sides with more than 1,400 monuments along a 16-mile (25km) route. More than 17,000 troops are buried in Vicksburg National Cemetery. There's also USS *Cairo* (raised from the depths), one of seven iron-clad gunboats that sailed the Mississippi.

Eventually the Louisiana bank gives way to Arkansas (the Arkansas River flows in) but the scenery, repeated swirls of flood plain where the river once used to curl, stays the same. The landscape is often best appreciated with the aid of a map – on the *American Queen* a 'riverlorian' holds sessions putting it all into perspective.

Some cruises call at Helena in Arkansas, small-town America that at one time was lost in a world of Interstates and shopping malls but has reinvented itself as a colourful, individual place.

The eastern bank gives way to Tennessee, with Memphis quickly appearing. Riverboats dock at modernistic Beale Street Landing, just along the road from live music haunts such as BB King's Blues Club. Many people finish (or start) their cruise with a stay here and who could argue. It was in Memphis, at Sun Studios, that Johnny Cash in 1958 recorded his love song to the Mississippi, 'Big River'.

Above left: The modern Memphis skyline seen from Mud Island River Park, reached by cable car

Right: Elvis Presley's Graceland mansion in Memphis and the statue of The King on the city's Beale Street, near the river

THE MISSISSIPPI
MEMPHIS TO ST LOUIS
A wild world between two sophisticated cities

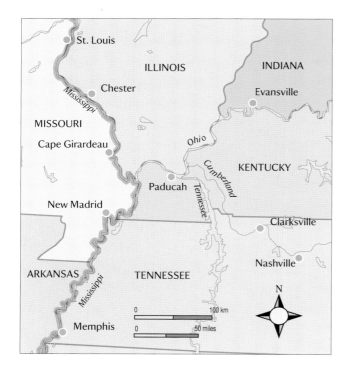

For most cruise passengers the stretch between Memphis and New Orleans (see pages 114-119) IS the Mississippi yet the true adventure begins when you head north from the home of Elvis. The river becomes ever wider and more indistinct, a swathe of water that rises and falls going where it sees fit with little regard for river banks and property. Over the centuries communities have been washed away by the relentless waters and nowadays few still exist close by the river. Those that do aren't simply protected by levees as farther south but also by high, prison-like walls. This is the land you imagine when reading *Huckleberry Finn*, a Mark Twain world that was the bringer of wealth with the steamboats but also destruction from the huge waters.

All that seems so far away in Memphis, an easy stroll from the innate southern style of the Peabody Hotel, where ducks still paddle in the lobby fountain. A must for any cruise-goer is Mud Island, just along from Beale Street Landing (with its spiralling gangways to account for the huge tidal rise and fall). Reached by a short-but-sweet monorail, it's home to the Mississippi River Museum (with everything from ship relics to an Elvis exhibit), and the 2,000ft (610m) re-creation of 954 miles (1,528km) of the river that pours out into the 'Gulf' with swan-shaped boats.

As the river heads north, civilisation is swiftly left behind for a landscape that could easily be mistaken for the Amazon, with its forests and little island beaches, where there is often no real dividing line between water and land; at times you feel that you could be at sea, gazing at the coast. The river then passes vast open spaces such as Chickasaw National Wildlife Refuge, where thousands of

migrating birds congregate in winter, away from any hint of population.

First stop is New Madrid (pronounced Mad-rid), a tiny town in Missouri. Its little museum recounts how, in 1811, this was the hub of one of the river's most cataclysmic events. An earthquake, believed to have topped seven on the Richter Scale, caused the river to run backwards, and shocks were felt as far away as Washington DC.

Soon the river takes a sharp left, seemingly a tributary of the Ohio River that pours in, forming the Kentucky border, yet the scale is all relative.

Next is quaint Cape Girardeau. The main street, a mix of dusty antiques stores, cafés and brewpubs, is small-town Americana while, for the most part, views are restricted to the 12ft (3m) protective wall covered in a mural stretching hundreds of feet depicting town and river. Climb to Cape Rock Park, site of the 'Old Bridge', to see the waters – and pop into the museum for the panoramic photo of when the bridge was demolished in one mighty explosion in 2003 to make way for its replacement.

The dreamy voyage is for the most part on the *American Queen*, the river's most impressive steamboat – on occasion its twin cast-iron chimneys are winched into a

Below: The soaring Bill Emerson Memorial Bridge is a stark contrast to quaint Cape Girardeau nearby – get a great view from Cape Rock Park

Above: Due to the fluctuating river levels the *American Queen* is designed so that her smokestacks fold down to negotiate bridges

horizontal position to just make it under bridges. Cars sometimes appear on nearby roads but for the most part this is a mysterious part of America that people rarely see.

Farther along on the other bank is Chester, Illinois. Initially there's nothing to be seen but a landing and road that are both regularly under water, with the backdrop of a rugged bluff. Yet, safe at the top, is a rural town where Mark Twain, a pilot on the Mississippi from 1857 to the Civil War, is said to have stayed on several occasions.

Its big claim to fame is that, in 1929, cartoonist Elzie Segar created Popeye the Sailor Man. The cinema where Segar was a projectionist is now a Popeye museum and gift shop. There's a 6ft (2m) bronze statue of Popeye in Elzie C. Segar Memorial Park; if that's surreal, the one of Olive Oyl (part of a trail of cartoon characters) is even more so.

Little disturbs the riverbank, with untamed countryside largely on bluffs well away from the water. Cliff Cave County Park is a mix of woodlands, wetlands and rocky hills – plus a cave with a spring, used as a meeting point by trappers and Confederate soldiers.

And then the bright lights of St Louis start to appear – and the 630ft (192m) stainless-steel Gateway Arch soars into the sky. Cruise ships dock all but beneath the Arch, which sits in riverside Centennial Park. The nation's tallest monument and the world's tallest arch, it is a celebration of westward expansion but also of the river itself. Take a ride in a tiny, egg-shaped tram car that climbs up the inside and from the top the river is spread out beneath you, disappearing into the haze in either direction – an amazing aerial view that exists nowhere else along the Mississippi's entire journey.

This is very much a city of the river. At the water's edge you can walk the cobbled streets among the brick ware-houses of Laclede's Landing, a place that used to be at the throbbing heart of trade on the Mississippi and which is now a place packed with restaurants, bars and cafés.

Some cruises head north for a week-long voyage to Minneapolis while occasionally there is one that does the river to the full, Minneapolis to New Orleans (or vice versa). For most, however, St Louis is the place to spend a day or two and experience the Mississippi from all angles.

Top: The statue of Popeye, one of a number in Chester, Illinois, celebrating the cartoon character's creation here in 1929

Above: Gateway Arch in St Louis, a stainless steel viewpoint from which one can see the Mississippi disappearing in either direction

THE ST JOHNS

Meandering gently through the Sunshine State

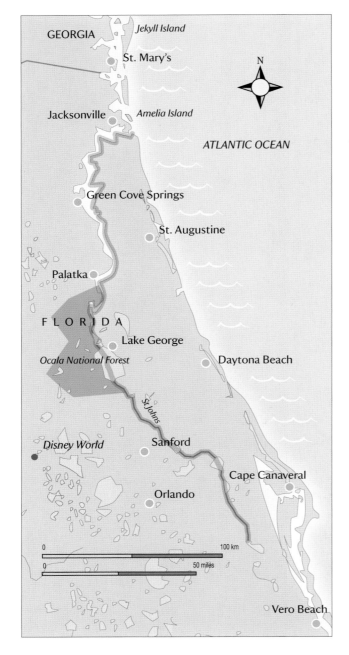

GEORGIA

Jekyll Island

St. Mary's

Jacksonville

Amelia Island

ATLANTIC OCEAN

N

Green Cove Springs

St. Augustine

Palatka

F L O R I D A

Lake George

Ocala National Forest

Daytona Beach

St Johns

Disney World

Sanford

Cape Canaveral

Orlando

0   100 km

0   50 miles

Vero Beach

Right: Dames Point Bridge crosses the river where it divides in two in Jacksonville, hopping on to Bartram Island in the middle

This is the river of the sun, flowing ever so gently northwards through Florida, often only a handful of miles from the east coast that it follows. While it can be overlooked as a major river, St Johns nevertheless travels 310 miles (500km) from swampland to the west of Vero Beach (south of the theme parks of Orlando) and enters the sea at Jacksonville, Florida's largest city.

Sluggish and with no real drop, only 30ft (9m) over its entire length, this is the original lazy river. The early stretches of the St Johns owe much to the Florida Everglades, flowing through trees with its banks sketchy; it's a place of airboat rides, and where manatees and alligators swim, where turtles and snakes live amongst the half-submerged trees. The river passes through many lakes, some of them tiny, a number of them not, not least Lake George, Florida's second largest, some 13 miles (22km) long.

It's the stretch between Jacksonville and Lake George that opens itself up to cruises. Where the river meets the sea is Everglade-like, with headlands and intricate waterways in Timucuan Ecological and Historic Preserve, home also to Kingsley Plantation, the state's oldest plantation house. Jacksonville is a place to appreciate the river in its sub-tropical warmth, with lengthy riverwalks on both banks taking in parks and the city's noted collection of mid-century modern architecture — Jacksonville Landing on the south bank is the place to eat and drink, particularly in the early even as the setting sun illuminates the water.

Channels go off in all directions in the city proper, with islands and yacht docks, yet this is a major river, one that morphs into a lake-like presence after rolling under a trio of bridges. It swiftly becomes several miles wide with bays and snaking inlets.

The city thins out and the river narrows down again, rolling through idyllic neighbourhoods and past waterfront mansions. This was a place that gunboats patrolled during the Civil War, and which was a major tourist route before

the coming of first the railroads and then the main roads nearer the heady attractions of the coast.

Cruises, on small, modern craft carrying maybe 100 passengers, call at charming towns such as Green Cove Springs and Palatka, both with historic downtowns that find their way to the river. At Green Cove Springs, Bayard Conservation Area, a place of huge cypress trees, deer and birds such as herons, hugs the river, still several miles wide. At Palatka the river is less than half as wide, the waters curling around the greenery of Horseshoe Point, another idyllic protected spot on a bend.

From here it's more a place of ranchland and forest, having veered away from the coast. The river rounds Drayton Island as it enters the lake, with Lake George Conservation Area hugging the east bank and Ocala National Forest stretching away on the other side. It's a tranquil place, one steeped in history — with steamboats of more than a century ago reaching here and doing a circuit before heading back to Jacksonville.

Often cruises on the St Johns also take in stretches of the Intracoastal Waterway, the natural passageways that circle the US, with darts up to the laid-back charms of Amelia Island and down, amongst communities and national parks, to the city of St Augustine.

THE ST LAWRENCE
The wild east coast, and whales too

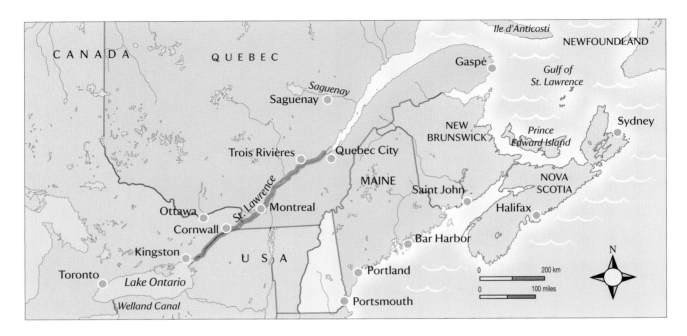

Sitting at a window in the castle-like Fairmont Le Château Frontenac hotel in the chill midwinter you realise what a grand river the St Lawrence is. Despite being in sophisticated Quebec City, the river is covered with icebergs, which charge first one way, then the other with the tidal surge. And during Winter Carnival there's perhaps the greatest river race of all as teams of canoeists paddle the waters and then scramble over the ice to be first ACROSS the river.

The river is the connection between the Great Lakes of North America and the Atlantic, flowing 750 miles (1,200km) from Lake Ontario. It starts as the border between Ontario and New York State then flows through Ontario and Quebec, taking in Montreal. Only around 300 miles (500km) is the river itself as shortly after Quebec City it becomes the Gulf of St Lawrence, the world's largest estuary, an ever-widening body of water which feels increasingly like the sea.

As such the St Lawrence offers cruising on both ocean and river vessels. The largest of ocean cruise ships from

Right: The annual race across the ice floes in Quebec City, with the Fairmont Le Château Frontenac looming in the background

mainstream companies regularly head up to Quebec City while small and mid-size ships can make it all the way to Montreal. It is also possible to find cruises that start in Manhattan, sailing the Hudson, taking the Erie Canal into the lakes then the St Lawrence all the way to the sea.

The river starts at the eastern shore of Lake Ontario near Kingston, Ontario, at the start of the Thousand Islands, an archipelago of 1,864 islands that stretch for 50 miles (80km). The largest is Wolfe Island, off Kingston, an ancient Mohawk hunting ground almost 20 miles (32km) long. It's a gentle, New England landscape that takes in the St Lawrence Seaway, a connected series of channels and locks that enable freighters to get between sea and lakes.

After the islands, the river narrows and straightens for a considerable time before expanding into another group of islands just before the town of Cornwall, where the US

border drops away. For around 30 miles (48km) it forms the Ontario-Quebec border before entering Quebec proper. The landscape is flat and fruitful although the river quickly changes again as it arrives at Grand Île. The main channel heads to the left, a tricky stretch of tiny islands and rapids, with the Beauharnois Canal slipping round to the right and south of the main river, which then flows into Lac St-Louis, a pretty body of water in Montreal. The waters narrow, drop south, fill out again and pass through the heart of the city, a cosmopolitan backdrop of glassy towers and classical French-influenced buildings.

Islands come and go before the river becomes Lac Saint-Pierre at the far end of which is the town of Trois-Rivières, named after the three strands of the Saint-Maurice River that join the St Lawrence. The streets of the town are lined with elegant historic buildings some of which date back to the 1700s.

Another 90 miles (145km) farther on and the river reaches Quebec City with its ancient stone quaysides lined with little restaurants serving moules-frites, the nearby Citadelle fortifications – and Fairmont Le Château Frontenac looming over everything.

The port area, a little farther on, where the St Charles River arrives, is breathtaking in its old city setting especially when the likes of Queen Mary 2 are docked. Several miles away is the 25-mile (40km) Île d'Orléans, a pastoral place with vineyards, walks, villages and quaint hotels. The river runs a good mile wide on either side of the island, coming together in a breathtaking waterway at least 10 miles (16km) wide, like an inland sea with hills and mountains rising on either side. Set back from the riverbank opposite the tip of the island is Mont-Sainte-Anne and a little farther on, running almost down to the river's edge, Le Massif, both ski resorts with sensational snowy views over river and valley through the winter.

By now we're effectively at sea with ships darting from place to place rather than simply making calls along a river.

As the gulf widens the chance of seeing marine wildlife becomes ever more likely, with the Saint Lawrence playing host to a number of species of whale including Sperm,

Minke and even the mighty Blue Whale. Many boat trips are available for close-up whale-watching. The town of Saguenay, at the mouth of the Saguenay fjord, is home to a large year-round colony of whales.

Baie-Comeau, close to the sea, is a place of wild Atlantic scenery where paper mills and logging are the main money makers, while the Manicouagan-Uapishka World Biosphere Reserve stretches away for miles; a rich, forested park following the Manicouagan river, a landscape forged by glaciers – and helped by a meteorite that left a circular lake.

Sept-Iles is a pretty little beach town with magnificent views across the St Lawrence to the mountains on the other side in the province of New Brunswick. The estuary widens even more, richer than ever in whales and birdlife. In the middle sits the Île d'Anticosti, a huntin' and fishin' paradise, but also somewhere from which you can explore in a sea kayak. Farther still, the estuary is protected by the island province of Newfoundland, although that's more than 100 miles (160km) away to start with, closing to 10 miles (16km) near the fishing community of Blanc-Sablon, wonderfully windswept with white sand beaches, and from where the ferry runs to Newfoundland. And that's about the end of the St Lawrence – the open sea beckons, with next stop the United Kingdom.

Left: Fairmont Le Château Frontenac stands tall above Quebec City, visible from the surrounding countryside

Below: Forge du St Maurice in Trois-Rivières, the first successful ironworks in 'New France', is a tourist attraction

THE YUKON

Tales of the Gold Rush across two countries

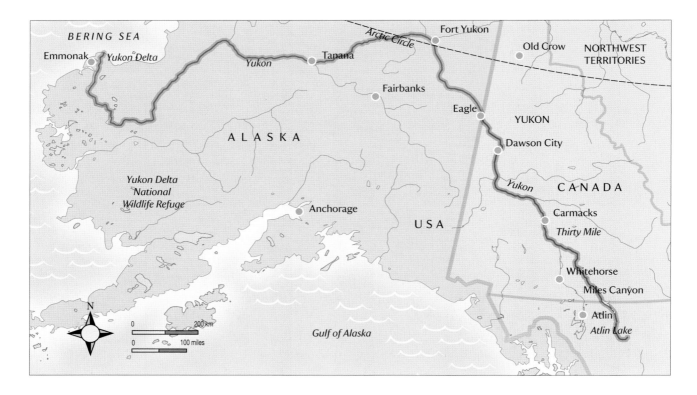

There's gold in them there hills, not to mention in the legends that surround this river that runs through rugged west coast Canada and into the US state of Alaska. This was a waterway that was central to the Klondike Gold Rush of 1896–1903 and one section in the Canadian province of Yukon, the 'Thirty Mile', from Lake Laberge to the Teslin River is a national heritage river and part of Klondike Gold Rush International Historical Park. Until the mid-20th century paddlewheelers made their way up the river, only letting off steam when the Klondike Highway opened.

The Yukon is generally said to start in Atlin Lake in British Columbia. From there it's almost 2,000 miles (3,200km) through Yukon Territory (named after the river) and across Alaska, until it finally tips into the Bering Sea.

Even today this is a place of adventure cruises on small passenger boats rather than major cruises from international operators. The river is navigable in stretches but

Right: Miles Canyon and its rugged basalt cliffs, between Atlin Lake and Whitehorse, can be explored by boat trip

splinters into striking yet problematical areas for long periods as it sweeps past mountains and glaciers, through forests and lakes under enormous skies. It is also the historic lifeline that links Alaskan communities such as Rampart and Russian Mission, Holy Cross and Fort Yukon.

The Yukon starts unassumingly enough as the Atlin River, wandering west from Atlin Lake near its southern end, and then makes its way north in parallel to the lake itself. Within no more than 60 miles (100km) of the northern tip of the latter it reaches Whitehorse, capital of the Yukon. To get here it has to pass through Miles Canyon, narrow and impressive with red basalt cliffs rising up from the azure waters and giving way to pine forest. As the river rounds a wide bend strewn with little islands, SS *Klondike* hoves into view. The largest of the sternwheelers of the British Yukon Navigation Company, she linked Whitehorse with Dawson City to the north. The grand old girl, pristine in white, now sits on the bank as part of a National Historic Site, alongside *Atlin*, built in 1934, the last of the wooden barges that used to ply this neck of the river.

The skies here are immense and the wilderness, laced with granity peaks, is reflected in the water. It's from here that boat trips head up river on MV *Schwatka*, a cute little thing that travels through Miles Canyon, so close that you can almost touch the rock walls, and into the expanse of Schwatka Lake, a reservoir created in the 1950s.

Novelist Jack London, whose masterpiece *The Call of the Wild* was set in the Klondike, travelled along the river when he came to try his fortune as a gold digger in 1897, alongside so many other hopefuls.

Whitehorse is the bright lights, a town of some 25,000 people, the biggest for a considerable distance. Barely 25 miles (40km) north of Whitehorse, the river opens out again into Lake Laberge, a body of water some 32 miles (50km) long and anything up to several miles wide; read all about it in Jack London's book. The north end of the lake is the start of the 'Thirty Mile', one of the most scenic stretches of the river. During the 1898 peak of the gold rush it's reckoned that up to 7,000 boats came through here carrying almost 30,000 gold diggers; it might have been scenic but it was a difficult stretch due to strong, shifting currents and rocks that could rip craft to shreds.

Today it is a place of recreation. Here are near-vertical bluffs reaching 330ft (100m), deep-sided tributaries rushing in and volcanic ash banks that resulted from an eruption 1,200 years ago. Grizzly Bears and Wolverines patrol the banks, Bald and Golden Eagles sail above. The river is full of salmon, as well as canoes, kayaks and rafts along with small power boats.

The nearest you'll get to a paddlewheeler these days is SS *Evelyn/Norcom* that has been gently decomposing on Shipyard (Hootalinqua) Island since being put into winter storage – in 1913. It's here, around the abandoned trading post of Big Salmon, where the Teslin River arrives from the east, that the Thirty Miles comes to an end.

You're so far north at this point that in the summer it's possible to marvel at the scenery under the midnight sun.

Above: Grizzly Bears are widespread – there are thought to be up to 7,000 in the Canadian part of the Yukon alone

Right: Dawson City, where Canada gives way to the wide-open expanse of Alaska, is a place for river trips

And there's no light pollution so that, from September onwards, the Northern Lights often appear, dancing through the skies.

The river passes tiny Little Salmon, once home to the Little Salmon/Carmacks First Nation, a tribe calling themselves the Big River People. Then it flows through the town of Carmacks, a village where many First Nation people now live and, on the Klondike Highway, one of only four places on the river where there's a road bridge. Low peaks follow the river in an area rich in coal, copper and gold while trucks rumble along the road. Shortly afterwards, huge bluffs on one side, views into seeming eternity on the other, is Five Finger Rapids, four islands creating five narrow channels, something to be braved on the way to the goldfields.

It's then more than 200 miles (240km) of wilderness before the last call for Canada, Dawson City. The river has become ever more difficult to navigate, islands and shingle banks forcing it into multiple channels. First the Pelly River rolls in from the mountains in the east then the

mile-wide (2km) White River from the west. Dawson has the feel of the pioneer town it was – timber buildings, dirt roads, and a little car ferry – surrounded by forested peaks. This was the heart of the gold rush, with a population of 40,000 at the end of the 19th century.

From here *Klondike Spirit*, defiantly the only paddle-wheeler still operating in Yukon, offers narrated, sightseeing journeys for up to 50 passengers.

It's still 130 miles (210km) to Alaska. On the way you pass Forty Mile, established in 1886, at the point where the Yukon and Fortymile Rivers meet, and now an historic site. First stop over the state line is tiny Eagle, little more than an historic district and a stop on the annual Yukon Quest

dog-sled marathon. From here there are rafting trips to Circle, 150 miles (240km) away, through Yukon-Charley Rivers National Preserve. Both were important towns in the late 1800s (Circle had an opera house) but the region is wilder now than even 50 years ago.

Once in Alaska there's still 1,400 miles (2,240km) to go before the river reaches the sea. From Circle it heads north into Yukon Flats National Wildlife Reserve. By the town of Fort Yukon – eight miles (13km) north of the Arctic Circle – it's not so much a river as a mass of channels many miles wide, packed with forested islands and lakes. This isn't a place for river cruises but it's still popular for rafting trips and camping on the banks in unblemished scenery. Bright

lights, such as they are, are restricted to spots such as Yukon River Camp, a charmingly understated diner/motel that sits by the Dalton Highway as it crosses the river.

From this point the river becomes more, well, river-like again, while still shallow and not given to cruises. There's a long way to go across beautiful, desolate landscapes, the tiny towns many miles apart, before entering Yukon Delta National Wildlife Refuge, a vast, eerily flat wetland, where the best part of two million ducks and geese make their home. The river wends its way north and past tiny fishing communities such as Emmonak and Alakanuk before emerging amongst rocky islands. The remoteness of the place makes it too far off the beaten track for river cruises.

The Orinoco runs the length of
Venezuela, through some of South
America's wildest scenery

South America

THE AMAZON
The biggest of them all

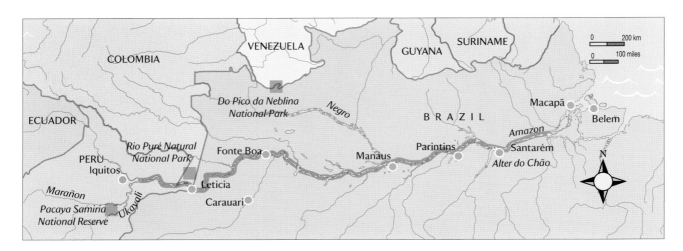

Generally rated the most awe-inspiring river system in the world, the Amazon is, depending who you're talking to, also the longest river (although the Nile still tries to stake its claim). It and its tributaries pass through not only the obvious Brazil (where you'll find most cruises) but also Peru, Bolivia, Colombia, Ecuador, Venezuela and Guyana. At its mouth, in Brazil, it is 125 miles (200km) wide, not recognisable as a river at all.

As such, cruising the Amazon comes in many guises. It's a river but not just a river, with ocean ships easily able to head to the gorgeous, colonial city of Manaus, almost 1,000 miles (1,600km) from the sea.

So it's a sea cruise, sometimes from South America, sometimes from the USA, sometimes even farther afield – UK company 'Cruise and Maritime Voyages' runs an annual 40-plus night voyage from Tilbury on the Thames to Manaus and back. Even 'river' cruises here, mostly on small steamers, tend to have more of a sea cruise feel with Manaus (once the rubber capital of the world) showing little sign of being a river destination.

Many voyages depart from Santarém, a small Brazilian city halfway between the Atlantic coast and Manaus. It's an area known as the Caribbean of Brazil, with more than 60 miles (100km) of beautiful white beaches. There's also

a tourist high point, with cruise ships anchoring near the fishing village of Alter do Chão, the Meeting of the Waters, where the clear waters of the Tapajós meet the muddy march of the Amazon, running alongside without merging for several miles, a place where both Pink River and Grey River Dolphins play. There are cruises from Santarém that navigate the lesser-visited stretch of the Amazon heading towards the gorgeous Portuguese colonial city of Belem, near the river's mouth; a gentle, small-boat experience.

But, again, this isn't a regular river and this is an experience like no other. The Amazon's tributaries pour in – the Ituqui, the Curua Una – and the lush rainforest, alive to the sight and sound of birdlife such as toucans and parrots, opens up to delights such as Lake Maica. Here motorboat excursions are often provided with crocodile spotting and even piranha fishing along with calls at remote villages to meet welcoming locals.

Farther on are the much-photographed stilt houses of the *caboclos*, the 'water people', descended from locals and their Portuguese conquerors in the 16th and 17th centuries. Near Lake Marai there might be a walking tour amid towering trees filled with monkeys and sloths as butterflies flit around in the hazy sunshine. On Lake Braganca you could find yourself watching the extravagant birdlife at

Below: The Meeting of the Waters, near Manaus, where the dark Rio Negro runs alongside the muddy Solimoes River

sunset. Boats also head for Lake Amorim on the Tapajós, while canoe excursions are something not to be missed.

Near Manaus is an even better known Meeting of the Waters. Tour boats leave the city for the spot where the black waters of the Rio Negro meet the yellow-brown of the Solimoes River, flowing side by side without mixing for about six miles (9km). It's impressive, rather like two differently coloured seas either side of a lush island. A trip here can also involve wandering the riverbanks, swimming and canoeing in lakes — and delving into the rich forest. Surprisingly to many, given the way we view the Amazon wilderness, there are half a dozen calls that cruise ships make aside from Santarém and Manaus. Parintins, second in size to Manaus and a third of the way there from Santarém (but still 350 miles/560km away), sits on Tupinambarana Island and gets busy with visitors for the Boi-Bumbá folklore festival each June. Between Santarém and Parintins, in particular, the Amazon drifts off into lagoons, is separated by islands and sandbanks, with vast lakes hidden behind precarious-looking pieces of land.

Alter do Chão itself is a village of stilted houses on a blue lagoon actually just in the Tapajós River. Locals here and elsewhere get about on canoes and other often home-made vessels. Another tiny settlement is Boca da Valeria, at the mouth of the Valeria River — more stilt houses in a picture-book setting backed by the rainforest.

Belém, close to the river's mouth but actually to one side of it on Guajará Bay, an ocean metropolis in pastel shades, was one of the first settlements on the Amazon, founded in 1616. It was a place for cultured highlife thanks to the rubber boom. Variously known as 'the tropical Paris' for its elegance and 'City of Mango Trees' for its exotic planting, its style is seen in the neoclassical Teatro da Paz built in 1874. Extravagant 17th- and 18th-century buildings are now museums while the buzzing Ver-o-Peso, by the bay, is the largest open-air market in Latin America, a place where it's impossible not to stop for a bag of freshly-shelled Brazil nuts as you marvel at the variety of fish piled high. The city snuggles behind a group of islands that protect it, with its palm-lined promenade, from the bay, which is up to 15 miles (24km) wide. The best time to come here is generally regarded as the 'dry' season, May to November, although it's all relative as the word 'rainforest' rather gives the game away. However, with the rains come more exciting waters, sometimes more than 20ft high, which all but take you into the jungle – closer to the monkeys, toucans and other exotic wildlife.

When you get to Manaus it's hard not to be surprised at the city that sits here in the middle of the jungle, a major

Ver-o-Peso market, with its cast-iron clocktower from England, stretches along the Belém waterfront

Above: The Teatro Amazonas opera house is one of many European-influenced extravagances in the city of Manaus, surrounded by jungle

port with all the elegance of Europe – the gold-domed Teatro Amazonas opera house, built of stone brought from Europe, and the Art Nouveau grandeur of the market hall, inspired by Les Halles in Paris.

You can't miss the city but neither should you miss a trip in a tiny boat into the placid backwaters, sometimes heading up waterways so narrow you can reach out and touch the trees that provide a canopy from the tropical sun.

Some smaller ocean ships head another 50 miles (80km) to UNESCO-protected Anavilhanas National Park along the Rio Negro. Around 400 islands create a mesmerising, untouched landscape some 80 miles (130km) long and more than 10 miles (16km) wide. In the river's meandering passageways you can see not only dolphins but also huge, lumbering manatees and alligators while the islands are home to jaguars, anteaters and armadillos. Tours take in beaches and offer treks amongst the flora.

This is an extraordinary region and, as the river grows ever wider, you'll never be sure when you've actually left it for the ocean.

ANOTHER AMAZON

It is also possible to cruise the Amazon in Peru, far away from the sea. Mostly the trips run from the city of Iquitos, 1,500 miles (2,400km) up river from Manaus, where the Rio Nanay joins the Amazon, and accessible only by river or air. There's a magical point 100 miles (160km) upstream where the Ucayali and Marañón Rivers meet and where the Amazon starts. It's a highlight of a cruise generally several days long and which is linked with visits to the capital, Lima, and the mountaintop city of Machu Picchu.

Iquitos, with a strong European heritage from its rubber-rich days, for the most part faces the Amazon yet also sits on a mile-wide lake. This itself turns into the Itaya River in the colourful district of Belen where stilt houses face the water and the teeming street market seems to go on forever. On the Amazon here, steamers in many states of existence ply the waters amongst the tour boats and skiffs in a colourful jungle scene.

Other expedition cruises, run by small specialists such as G Adventures, leave from Nauta, just on the Marañón. They explore the Amazon as a region rather than the river itself, delving into Pacaya Samiria National Reserve, an immense area of floodable forest sandwiched between the Marañón and Ucayali, where spider monkeys, three-toed sloths and giant South American Turtles exist alongside a vast bird population.

Below: Golden lion monkeys, tree frogs and macaws are just some of the species that fill the rainforest with colour... and noise

Bottom: The jaguar is king of the jungle in the Amazon, often found close to the riverbank commanding hot, marshy terrain

THE ORINOCO
Land of the piranha...

Right: The palms on the banks of the Orinoco suddenly part to reveal yet another village that stretches back generations

The romance of a river where you can fish for piranha is undeniable and simply the name, Orinoco, conjures up far-flung places, yet few people could pinpoint exactly where it is. From its source in the Guiana Highlands, the Orinoco actually stretches the length of Venezuela, running 1,330 miles (2,140km) into the Atlantic Ocean on the edge of the Caribbean, in the north-east corner of South America.

Christopher Columbus noted the river's mouth at the end of the 15th century, Sir Walter Raleigh sailed up the Orinoco at the end of the 16th century and yet it wasn't until the 1960s that the river was bridged, so far from civilisation is most of it.

The river starts on Venezuela's western fringes as a number of Colombian rivers come together in Parima Tapirapecó National Park. For the first 150 miles (240km) it pours out of the mountains, lush and tropical, into a no less lush flatland and forest with streams and small rivers everywhere, the river irrigating and overflowing wherever it goes. This section comes to an end at the rapids and falls of Raudales de Guaharibos.

From here it continues for hundreds of miles through mostly impenetrable rainforest or swathes of grassland. Few people travel here and the river is all but impossible to navigate as it runs through a series of rushing, rocky stretches, ending in the Atures Rapids. This is the opening of the Orinoco Basin and the river bends to the east, reaching up to five miles (8km) in width as tributaries continue to pour in.

Eventually the waters form a delta and what a delta it is, stretching 120 miles (190km) to the Gulf of Paría, all but an inland sea dividing Venezuela and the Caribbean island of Trinidad. When it reaches the sea the delta is more than 200 miles (240km) wide. The huge area is an extraordinary wetland ecosystem filled with jungle, lakes, endless tiny rivers and streams, and a wealth of animal and bird life.

The delta is the region where cruises and river trips can be found – although this is by no means a major cruise destination – as towns begin to appear and sandy islands become widespread. There's Ciudad Bolivar with its pastel-hued buildings; here the river slims to only a mile wide, the site of the Orinoco's first crossing, the Angostura suspension bridge, in 1967. Another 60 or so miles (100km) is Ciudad Guayana as the river splits into more channels; here the Caroni River joins the Orinoco and a short way up the Caroni are the impressive Llovizna Falls. Just upstream from Ciudad Guayana the sleek, modern Orinokia Bridge soars across the wide Orinoco. Opened in 2006, this is the river's second bridge. A little further there's the small town of Barrancas. The waters are wide and muddy, the scenery low and little boats buzz about.

The main channel, known now as the Río Grande, is shadowed by many more. It is an area of exotic wildlife... the Orinoco Crocodile, which can reach 20ft (6m), one of the world's biggest, the more delicate caimans, boa

There's a feeling of otherworldliness as elegant superyacht-like vessels sail slowly amid the dense, rich vegetation in places where the Pink River Dolphins break the water, and monkeys and macaws screech. Zodiac inflatables leave the ship to get even closer to both water and land. These outings are led by expert guides, along tiny tributaries such as the El Toro and to a tiny village of the same name. Grab a line baited with raw meat and see if the piranhas bite...

The people of the Warao tribes inhabit the delta, travelling silently and smoothly in simple wooden canoes, though some have outboard motors. Cruises often involve interaction with the locals, visiting villages where thatched huts sit on stilts to keep them above the ebb and flow of the waters.

The combination of cruise ship and small inflatable raft offers twin experiences essential for exploring an extraordinary landscape that has been all-but untouched for centuries. The journey ends at the sea where headlands — actually small islands divided by waterways — stand guard with small, lushly forested peaks, a sight of prehistoric wilderness that Christopher Columbus noted all those years ago.

constrictors, anacondas, turtles and manatees. The noise of howler monkeys and macaws echoes around and Pink River Dolphins leap into the warmth of the tropical air. Palm trees dot the banks before much bigger hardwoods loom up. Jaguars and pumas prowl in the undisturbed forest depths.

Motorboats buzz around while steamers provide an irregular service from the delta all the way to Atures Rapids, some 700 miles (1,100km) upstream. Mainstream cruise ships sometimes enter the delta — and ocean ships can navigate for around 250 miles (400km) — but tourist transport is more usually restricted to day trips on small craft, often canoes. These generally are part of an adventure that involves staying at one of the many remote lodges hidden in the rainforest along myriad tributaries.

However, luxury small cruise ships, such as those of the French Ponant company, are starting to venture into the Orinoco. These take in the river on cruises that dart around the Caribbean (the Orinoco Delta is no farther than other islands when you are in this part of the world) and toy with other South American calls.

Above left: The sleek, modern Orinokia Bridge, near Ciudad Guayana, was built in 2006, only the second crossing of the Orinoco

Above: The caiman is far smaller than the Orinoco crocodile, but just as much a threat should you fancy heading in for a swim

The sun-drenched Nile is fringed by greenery beyond which the desert forms a hypnotic backdrop

Africa

THE CHOBE
Some of the best big game spotting in the world

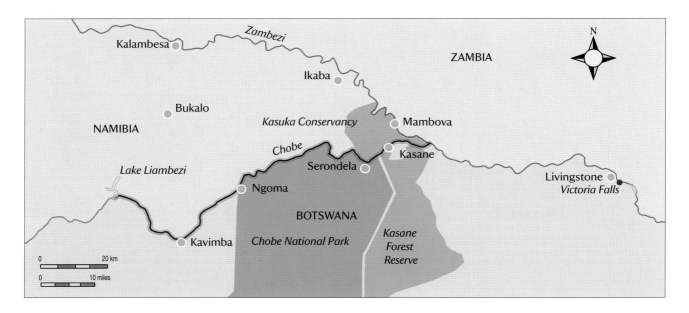

The Chobe is a boutique river by African standards. A tributary of the mighty Zambezi, the Chobe forms the Namibia-Botswana border for most of its true journey from Lake Liambezi before reaching the Zambezi at the point where the two nations all but come together with Zambia and Zimbabwe.

The river actually rises in Angola, as the Cuando, disappearing for a time into the Kalahari sands, and continues to the Linyanti swamp on the edge of Botswana, then, as the Linyanti, runs the Namibia-Botswana border to Lake Liambezi.

Yet of the 450-mile (720km) run, it's only the final 15-mile (25-km) stretch of the Chobe itself that is on the cruise radar, passing between Chobe National Park, one of Africa's finest parks, and the Kasika Conservancy (more of the same with lots of help for local people). And this is Africa as you imagine it, dusty plains stretching into the distance, spotted with low, bushy trees, and wildlife pottering about with barely a care in the world.

The river is small – it's not a major artery and there are no big ships here. Cruises are typically several days on tiny but luxurious houseboats such as the well-established *Zambezi Queen*, with 14 suites, and, launched at the end of 2017, the *African Dream* for only 16 guests. Smaller still are three *Chobe Princesses*, rather like floating apartments, two of which sleep only eight guests. All combine contemporary design with African motifs.

Chobe National Park has one of Africa's biggest concentrations of game but is famed for its elephant and buffalo. There are believed to be 40,000 to 60,000 elephants, so they are everywhere, whether you are on a safari day trip or on the river. In the dry season – generally May to early November – they line the banks and wander through the shallow waters all but oblivious to the gawping tourists. Giraffe, wildebeeste and antelope also make their presence felt with only the prowling leopards, cheetahs, wild dogs and lions to spoil the party, although many stray farther afield.

Most cruises are extensions of longer, more far-reaching tours, involving stays in safari lodges (such as the riverfront Ichingo, part of the *Zambezi Queen* set-up) and often stays in cities such as Johannesburg. The Okavango Delta, some 150 miles (240km) south-east across the veldt, is a network of waterways where game drives and night adventures are held.

Cruises on the Chobe aren't journeys with regular stops and a start and a finish. It's not so much a regular schedule; it's more pottering up and down to find the best of the animal magic that day, in conjunction with other activities. You'll find that the boats have even smaller boats so you can fish (catfish, African pike and more) or simply pootle amongst the submerged (and easily annoyed) hippos and ever-watchful crocodiles, sometimes down on to the Zambezi. There are also game drives and excursions to local villages.

The scenery doesn't change greatly but then why should it? This is lazing in the heart of Africa and you have the world's most wondrous wildlife flocking around you. Simply sit on the sundeck and make the most of it.

Bottom: *Zambezi Queen* wanders up and down a short stretch of the Chobe looking for the best wildlife – and a perfect sunset

Below: Elephants are widespread along the stretches of the Chobe and there's the chance to get up close by small boat

THE CONGO

A mighty route through the heart of Africa

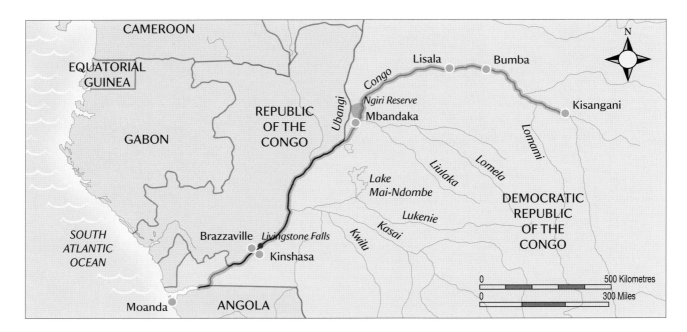

This is one of Africa's mightiest rivers, second only to the Nile in length, and deep and wide with it. From its source in the mountains by the Zambian border (there known as the Lualaba River) it flows north through the Democratic Republic of the Congo (DRC) then west through neighbouring Republic of the Congo and into the sea back in the DRC. On its near 3,000-mile (4,800km) route it passes through the Congo rainforest (surpassed in size only by the Amazon), through pools and canyons, and through many lakes. The capitals of both countries, Kinshasa in the former and Brazzaville in the latter, face each other across an extremely wide stretch of river.

And yet this beautiful wilderness isn't a place for mainstream cruises; in parts it is anything but navigable, a stretch of more than 200 miles (320km) running east of the DRC capital, Kinshasa, being a succession of narrow rapids, known as the Livingstone Falls, during which the river drops a good 900ft (275m). It is possible, however, to find varied expedition-style trips through tour operators, with lots of local operations too.

A popular option is the 700-mile (1,000km) stretch farther inland between Mbandaka and Kisangani. This isn't sexy, modern stuff; you'll find yourself travelling in open, wooden boats around 100ft (30m) long. The journey is divided between two 10–12 day segments, with the town of Lisala in the middle, with riverside camping and the occasional small hotel.

While the river is a lifeline, it passes through harsh and largely deserted places, long stretches where the bleak beauty of Africa shines through. Mbandaka was founded (as Équateurville), like many places in these parts, by explorer Henry Stanley. It's the closest city in the world to the equator (a couple of miles) and the Equator Stone Stanley placed at the point the line was believed to cross the river is still here. Head north and there are vast areas of swamp forest, much in the Ngiri Reserve, with the river flowing in many channels between islands and sandbanks with only occasional settlements.

The journey often involves little more that sitting back and letting the wide open expanse of Africa pass by, along with fishing boats and the occasional very basic ferry. Stops involve buying food from markets and traders, and being the centre of attention in spots whose inhabitants see few outsiders. Communities include Makanza, a colonial trading post from the late 19th century. Lisala is a pretty, colonial place dominated by the Cathédrale Saint-Hermès.

The second stretch passes the Maringa-Lopori-Wamba landscape, one of Africa's poorest areas, where crops such as maize are farmed and conservationists attempt to limit the slash-and-burn mentality that clears the forest in an effort to create more farmland.

On the opposite bank is Bumba, a ramshackle port town, near where the river is at its widest, at 12 miles (20km), and often a sea of water hyacinths. Nearing Kisangani the river slides placidly through the Yangambi Biosphere Reserve, tropical forests where 32,000 tree species have been identified and where elephants, river hogs and monkeys can be spotted.

Kisangani (originally Stanleyville, named after good old Henry Stanley) is the end of the navigable stretch of the river. This is a city of European-style buildings, not least the Cathédrale Notre-Dame du Rosaire, and has a lively centre.

Right: The Congo passes through a massive rainforest but in many areas it is navigable only by small, traditional craft

THE NIGER

From the Sahara to the sea, via Timbuktu

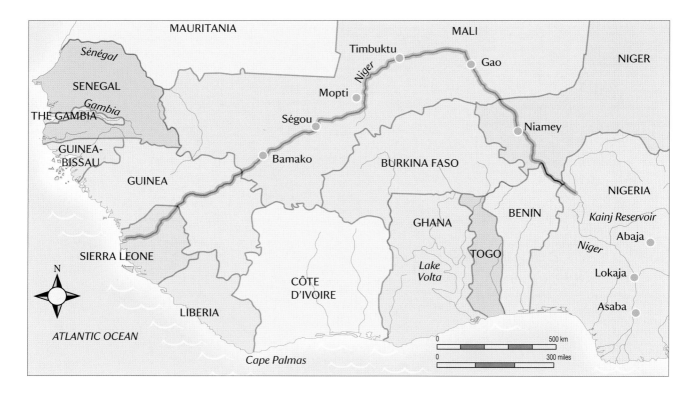

The Niger River sweeps in a giant arc of 2,600 miles (4,300km) across western Africa into the Atlantic. It starts in the highlands of Guinea, curves north through Mali (which accounts for almost half its length), into Niger, then forms the border of Niger and Benin before heading south through Nigeria, disappearing in the giant Niger Delta. Yet despite its length, the river is both difficult to navigate due to its unruly route and is well off most tourist paths as it passes through dry, dusty wilderness.

Despite emerging only 150 miles (240km) from the sea its path takes it into the Sahara, skirting the city of Timbuktu. It's this section, in Mali, that is both fascinating and has a tourist set-up, even if this is far from the luxurious game camps in other parts of Africa. Here the scenery turns from baked to green and pleasant almost overnight thanks to the rainy season and the floods that transform the Niger itself into something that can reach several miles

wide in places. Most cruises from local companies such as West Africa Tours, sail between the colourful city of Timbuktu, on the edge of the Sahara, surrounded by dunes which drift into the streets, and Mopti, to the south-west.

Mopti, 250 miles (400km) away, becomes a series of causeway-linked islands during August-December when floods follow the rainy season. The river, and the port of Kabara, is 10 miles (16km) south of the city but is connected by canal.

No luxury cabins here — nights are spent in makeshift, yet evocative, camps on the riverbank. Other local companies such as Saga Tours run trekking/river holidays with several days sailing in a small boat between Mopti and Segou farther into the Inner Niger Delta, where the climate switches from arid to rainy from June to September.

Segou is a sizeable town, with a mix of French Colonial and African architecture, all mosques and grand buildings, while a 17th-century village of the same name sits just along the river. The soft adventure trips take in fishermen's villages and the camps of desert nomads, gently passing hippos and varied birdlife in a setting that is all-but desert. Again, nights are spent camping on the riverbank with very basic facilities but with a real feeling of being at one with the African continent.

For the very adventurous, steamer ferries run during high water season (mid-August to late November) between Koulikoro (near Mali's bustling capital, Bamako) in the south-east and Gao, some 875 miles (1,400km) north-east. The Mopti-Timbuktu stretch in the middle operates slightly longer.

The full ferry journey takes about a week, with frenetic stops at a host of villages. There are cabins and even a meal service but, packed with locals and cargo, this is an option for backpackers. It is also possible to find places on a *pinasse*, a large dugout canoe with motor, that is used as very basic public transport.

Nigeria, meanwhile, in early 2017 announced that it had completed the dredging of a 350-mile (570km) stretch of the Niger all the way from the Atlantic, which could lead to more river trips making their unhurried way into the country's isolated interior.

Bottom: The Niger makes a giant curve through western Africa, an off-the-beaten-track journey that is only for the adventurous

Below: A haphazard street market takes place in front of the Great Mosque of Djenné, in the Mopti region

THE NILE

The pyramids, the temples – and plenty of desert

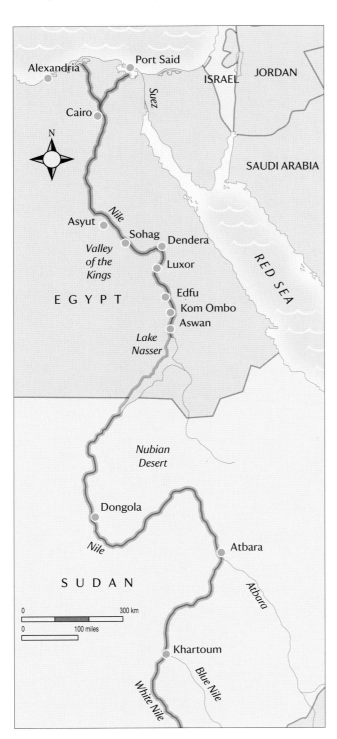

At more than 4,000 miles (6,400km), the Nile is the longest river in Africa – some say the world – but although it flows through 11 countries, most people associate it with Egypt, where it drains into the Mediterranean. Lake Victoria (mostly in Tanzania and Uganda but which also forms the border with Kenya), is generally said to be the main source of the Nile – although it's also agreed that there are several.

What is undisputed is that it's a very impressive river, so immense that it has two sections: the White Nile, which starts at Lake Victoria, and the Blue Nile, which comes from Lake Tana in Ethiopia. They meet in Sudan, the country directly south of Egypt, to form a wide river that is the main source of water for both countries – its floodlands being their main agricultural area.

Steamers can navigate the Nile where it passes through Lake Albert, on the border of Uganda and the Democratic Republic of the Congo. In South Sudan it flows through narrow gorges and rapids, with no navigable sections, and in the north of Sudan it drains into Lake Nasser, the massive reservoir that straddles Sudan and Egypt.

The lake was created when Aswan High Dam was built in Egypt, between the 1950s and early 1970s. It replaced the original Aswan Dam, which wasn't strong enough to stop the Nile from flooding every year and washing away crops, and it provides electricity across Egypt.

Cruises on Lake Nasser are an alternative to those on the Nile, the main attraction being the Ramesses II Temple and smaller Queen Nefertari Temple at Abu Simbel, both cut into blocks and rebuilt above the waterline when the dam, several miles south of Aswan itself, flooded the valley. The two 13th-century BC temples were hewn out of the cliffs in ancient Nubia, five miles (8km) from Sudan, with four colossi of Ramesses II guarding the door to the spectacular Sun Temple and six equally large statues outside Nefertari's Temple. Also rescued was the Temple of Isis at Philae, which stands on an island three miles (5km) from Aswan.

Aswan to Luxor, about 125 miles (200km) downstream, is the main section for cruises, with some going farther north to Dendera. Traditional wooden *felucca* sailing boats with local crews can be hired for a few hours or days at a time. A dozen or so passengers can sit on a carpet and cushion-strewn deck, sleeping on deck for longer journeys with food either brought from nearby villages or cooked on the sandy river banks next to fields of wheat, rice and sugarcane.

River cruise ships, taking 100 passengers or so, also travel between Aswan and Luxor, a journey that takes a few days although most itineraries make a week out of it in order to give time for sightseeing.

In Aswan's Nubian Museum the photos of UNESCO's rescue of Abu Simbel and Philae Temple will leave you desperate to visit the sites — Abu Simbel is reached by a small aircraft flight or long coach journey while Philae is easily accessible on a day's cruise of Lake Nasser.

Perfect for afternoon tea or a sunset cocktail is the Old Cataract Hotel, where English thriller writer, Agatha Christie, wrote part of *Death On The Nile*. The Victorian-built, colonial-style hotel has Moorish arches, Persian carpets and gardens that drift down to the river. From Aswan — don't miss the Sharia al-Souq market — you can take a trip to Elephantine Island and its Aswan Museum, then a row-boat to Aswan Botanical Gardens — an island still known as

Left: The Ramesses II Temple is guarded by a row of colossal statues carved from the rock of the mountain setting

Above: Traditional *felucca* sailboats, a great way to see the Nile, slice through the placid waters near the city of Aswan

Kitchener's Island after Lord Kitchener of Khartoum, Britain's Viceroy of Egypt.

Kom Ombo is the first stop after Aswan, with a Greco-Roman double temple dedicated to the crocodile god, Sobek, and falcon-headed god, Horus. Crocodiles used to live in the Nile and mummified crocodiles can still be seen in the temple sanctuary. Kom Ombo was once on the Nubian caravan routes, which included various gold mines, and, like other temples, the walls and columns are carved with kings, queens, gods and hieroglyphics.

Edfu, farther along, is one of the best-conserved temples despite being abandoned in 1 AD when Roman rulers banned non-Christian religions. It became buried under

silt from floods and shifting sand so that by 1798 only the
highest part was visible. In 1860 work began to uncover
the temple and its carved walls now rise so tall it makes
visitors feel tiny.

The Temple of Khnum at Esna is much smaller because
most of its buildings are still covered with silt and sand —
and the homes that were built on top. Being much lower
than the town's streets, it looks like it's part of an archaeological dig. Esna town, also on the caravan routes, features
Fatimid minaret, one of Egypt's oldest, and cafés where
you can sip mint tea and watch horses and carts go by.

The river, big as it is, isn't hugely wide and it meanders
through its lush flood plain, where trees and other
greenery form a barrier between the Nile and the vast
desert. Villages and towns appear lush, with plenty of
brightly coloured flowers, and farmland stretches for several miles.

Luxor is the next stop. Visiting Luxor Temple in the middle of town is simple and from here you can walk down the
extraordinary avenue of sphinxes to Karnak Temple a mile
away. Karnak Temple is a massive complex, and best not to
be attempted on the same day — although you can see it

from a different viewpoint at the evening Sound & Light shows.

This is the town from where you visit the Valley of the Kings and the Valley of the Queens, the burial sites of the pharaohs near the ancient city of Thebes, from around 2000 BC. Of more than 60 pharaoh tombs in the Valley of the Kings alone only a fraction are open to visit – and Tutankhamun's tomb is an additional fee.

The tomb of Ramses VI has intricately coloured drawings on the walls, ceiling and columns of the chambers and Queen Tausert's tomb is fascinating as she was the only woman to rule Egypt as a pharaoh. The Valley of the Queens has at least 75 tombs, with only a few open to view – Nefertari is the most famous.

The Colossi of Memnon, a 60ft (18m) sandstone statue, sits on the road between Luxor and the valleys.

Another day trip on the river from Luxor is to the Temple of Hathor at Dendera, 37 miles (60km) north and on the western bank opposite Qena. Dating back to just 125 BC, it is unusual in still having a ceiling. Dedicated to Hathor, the goddess of love, it also has a panel carved with a picture of Cleopatra and her son Caesarion.

From here it's still almost 400 miles (640km) to Cairo, but the stretch isn't as rich in antiquities. There is, however, Abydos, a major burial ground for Egyptian royalty believed to be the entrance to the underworld, where Abydos Temple can be visited. Amarna, on the east bank, is the abandoned ancient capital of Akhetaten, originally housing temples, royal palaces, residential homes and shops – now just ruins.

Cairo is an assault on all your senses; it's noisy, hot and insanely busy but a visit to the pyramids and huge Sphinx statue as you arrive at the southern suburb of Giza is practically compulsory. While you might picture them as in the desert, these wonders of the world are close to houses, restaurants and shops, which somehow makes the sight of these burial complexes even more breathtaking. You can pay to enter some of them but the steep, narrow tunnels to the inner chamber are not for the faint-hearted.

The Grand Egyptian Museum houses more than 100,000 artefacts including part of the Sphinx's beard. Many

artefacts were previously housed in the famed Egyptian Museum at Tahrir Square, where the standout highlight has for decades been Tutankhamun's treasures.

The river is imperious as it cuts through the city, a sprawling mix of beauty and chaos; smart hotels and apartments line some areas but the crazy, half-finished buildings sit alongside far more historic spots. Not to be missed is Aqsunqur Mosque, also known as the Blue Mosque, and the Museum of Islamic Ceramics on Gezira Island.

From Cairo the Nile spreads into the Nile Delta and out to the Mediterranean, the delta covering 150 miles (240km) from Alexandria in the west to Port Said in the east. In Alexandria there are Greek and Roman ruins, modern museums and sandy beaches, while at Port Said the elegant Suez Canal Authority Building marks out the city as the entrance to the canal that connects the Med to the Red Sea. It's a city of African, Arabian and European influences – a fitting mix for the end to a fascinating journey.

Above: The Nile is bordered by lush vegetation and farms with deserts and mountains providing a spectacular backdrop

THE SENEGAL
A voyage through colonial history

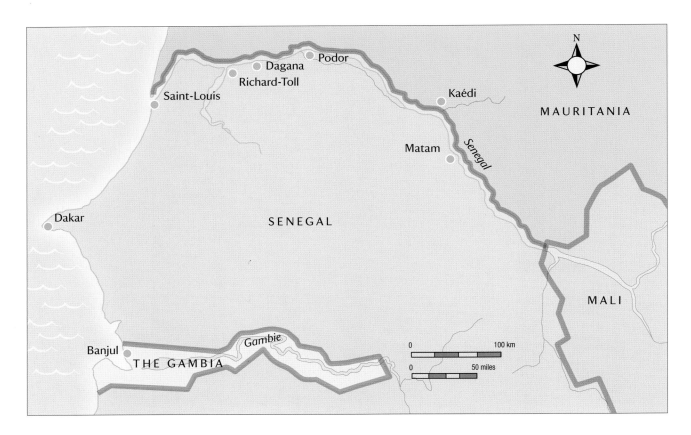

A river journey that has the spirit of Graham Greene or W. Somerset Maugham, in pale linen suit and Panama hat, sitting on the deck of a travel-worn ship sailing through a world that combines colonial grandeur and the breathtaking expanse of the Sahara Desert.

The Senegal River forms the border between Senegal itself and Mauritania to the north, in Western Africa. It actually emerges in Mali before making its way west but it is the stretch between the Atlantic Coast, at the city of Saint-Louis, and the town of Podor that is of interest, with a trip aboard *Bou el Mogdad*. As far back as 1950 the ocean-going ship was transporting mail, food and more to French trading posts. Reborn in 2005, it has since been running weekly cruises. White painted with red trim on the outside, a calm world of polished wood on the inside, it carries 54 passengers in unassuming comfort complete with small pool, bars, even a library.

Saint-Louis is large and cosmopolitan across three areas: the mainland; the Langue de Barbarie spit that extends for eight miles (13km), dividing the river from the sea, where there are long beaches; and the old town on N'Dar Island, linked to the mainland by Gustave Eiffel's 1865 Faidherbe Bridge.

The river is wide, the scenery low as the ship heads inland and through the lock of the Diama Dam, passing nature reserves and reaching Djoudj National Bird Sanctuary, a UNESCO World Heritage Site, whose wetlands teem with more than 1.5 million birds including flamingos and white pelicans. The scenery changes little, except to become drier and harsher, albeit studded with stylish

extravagances, both buildings and gardens, created by the French over the past couple of centuries. Richard-Toll features the near-derelict Château de Baron Roger, created with its gardens for the French governor in 1822.

The banks of the river on the Senegal side are irrigated and produce huge amounts of rice and sugar. Across the placid waters the true desert landscape becomes apparent.

In Dagana, once an important trading post, the riverbanks are near and sand-coloured dock buildings speak of its former importance, while nearby the market is a ramshackle affair in the dirt road.

The town of Podor is another old trading post, site of a dilapidated French fort, the pale stone buildings along the river reflected serenely in the tranquil waters.

Above: *Bou el Magdad*, a ship with the feel of a classic past, sits alone in the empty, mesmerising scenery in the west of Africa

The journey on the *Bou el Magdad* offers immersion into the local communities with visits to schools, markets and far-flung villages. Walk along the water's edge as washerwomen do their work and animals — cattle, varieties of antelope and even wild boar — come down to drink. The ship's tender takes tours to little backwaters in what becomes an increasingly remote and cut-off region as you travel upriver. Yet the mix of 13th-century settlements and the style of the French former rulers is intriguing, offering a river journey that is considerably different from much of Africa.

THE ZAMBEZI
Elephants, lakes – and Victoria Falls

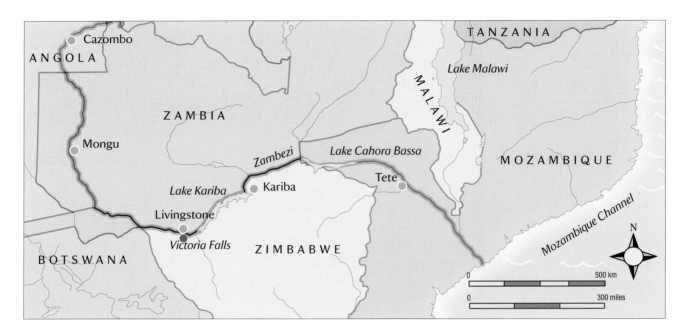

The Zambezi starts in the boggy wilds of northern Zambia, cuts through Angola then back into Zambia. It then follows the Namibian border, clipping Botswana before tracing the Zambia-Zimbabwe border (taking in 150-mile Lake Kariba) and plunging through Mozambique to the Indian Ocean. It stretches 1,600 miles (2,575km) yet is still only the fourth longest river in Africa.

As rivers go, it is one of the most difficult to navigate being a curious mix of shallows, narrows, channels and even white water. And yet it is possible to take to the river, even if only for relatively short stretches. It's not somewhere for long, scenic cruising as in some parts it's impossible to sail, with rapids and rocks, and even where small boats can settle on the shallow waters, it divides, often depending on the season, making it difficult to find a path.

Things are also hampered somewhat by Victoria Falls, the river at its grandest plunging over a cliff to form the widest waterfall in the world. It's a special place, awe-inspiring views across the 'smoke that thunders' as the falls are known locally.

Here, on the stretch of river above the falls, is one of the best (and most organised) spots to see the Zambezi's delights. It's wide but hard to reconcile as a river, looking more like a lake dotted with lush, tree-covered islands. Wildlife is abundant, with elephants and much more.

Two local companies – Zambezi Explorer and Shearwater – offer cruises that mostly settle on a time of day, often with food, such as sunrise, lunch, sunset and dinner, and are often packaged with guided walks and helicopter flights. If you're here, you'll want to see the river, the falls and the surrounding scenery from as many angles as possible.

At the bottom of the falls you can canoe, swim and enjoy other water sports, but from here the river, known as the Middle Zambezi, starts a journey between vertical rock walls, including Batoka Gorge, one of the world's most challenging whitewater stretches.

After more than 120 miles (190km) the river is calmed by Lake Kariba. This inland sea is the world's largest man-made lake, 175 miles (280km) long and up to 25 miles

Below: Batoka Gorge, a short way downstream from Victoria Falls, is a churning mass of whitewater between forbidding rock walls

(40km) wide. Houseboat holidays are popular with the occasional small cruise-boat such as 44-person *Southern Belle* offering overnight stays. Wildlife can be spotted around the 1,250 miles (2,000km) of shore, with hippos and the many crocodiles making it inadvisable to dip your toe in the enticingly warm waters.

From here it's about 100 miles (160km) to the river's other popular stretch where Zambia's Lower Zambezi National Park sits on one bank, Zimbabwe's Mana Pools National Park on the other. Yet again, this is only a place for small boat trips, but is busy with kayakers. River trips largely take place on rather engaging, flat-bottomed craft with an outboard motor that can get up a fair lick of speed, exhilarating as they bank and dash down narrow channels in search of the best of the wildlife. Most operate from lodges and get out amongst the elephants and hippos, often able to get up close to lions and leopards on the bank, as well as bobbing amongst birdlife such as the colonies of herons and the multi-coloured bee-eaters.

Above and below: Hippos are widespread and you're more likely to see a canoe than larger boats due to the shallow waters

Right: The dam, set amongst canyon walls, that holds in the mighty lake of Cahora Bassa as the river enters Mozambique

From every angle the backdrop changes, hills and low, dusty peaks in the distance, forested swathes and the dust and the sun, like a scene from *Out Of Africa*. Here you feel at one with nature, the dusty floodplains and oxbow lakes alive with elephants, which swim across the sandy water to grassy islands to feed alongside the buffalo. The Lower Zambezi Valley chops and changes, at times the backdrop of lush mountains and hills coming in close, at others thick forests taking charge before grasslands take over. It's difficult to know what to *ooh* and *aah* at first – zebra, wildebeest, elegant impala and other dancing, prancing game. Kingfishers are the least exotic of the bird life, while there are regular incursions by lions, leopards and wild dogs.

This meandering and sometimes wide stretch goes on for maybe 65 miles (95km) and is lined by a succession of idyllic game lodges and camps – this tends to be the way to see the river, a holiday here that is land-based luxury with a combination of safaris and river excursions. Trips take place from the likes of Chongwe, Chiawa and Sausage

Tree camps on the northern bank, as well as Ruckomechi across in the Mana Pools area of Zimbabwe.

The river slims down for a long stretch but as it enters Mozambique it opens into the expanse of Cahora Bassa, another dammed stretch. This is 160 miles (250km) long and up to 24 miles (38km) wide, much of it calm and open but becoming a rocky canyon as it nears the dam. Like so much, this is remote and there are no regular cruises but lodges, such as Ugezi Tiger Lodge, are springing up. These offer boat trips, either purely sightseeing, some going down to the mighty dam itself, or for angling as the lake is full of dozens of varieties of fish, including eel and catfish.

After this the river makes its way across Mozambique to the Zambezi Delta where, a few miles from the sea, it divides, creating Ilha Pambane. This is swampland, home to some Africa's biggest buffalo, yet, a place away from the tourist trail. One of the world's most diverse wetlands, where pelicans and flamingoes live alongside elephants, lions and leopards, it is almost impenetrable.

A tiny traditional craft plies the Ayeyarwady in
a mystical setting near Mandalay

Asia

THE AYEYARWADY

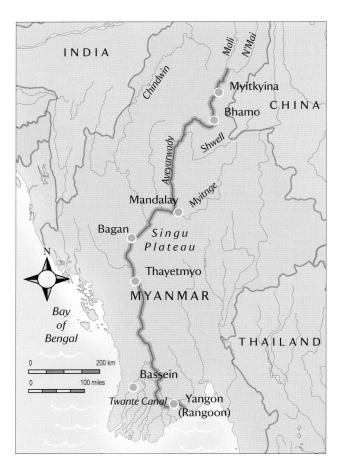

Right: The mountains of Myanmar's north give way to gentler scenery, a fertile landscape offering sensual sunsets

From the Northern Mountains at the very tip of Myanmar (the former Burma), the Ayeyarwady (previously called the Irrawaddy) runs though a mystical, timeless landscape due south through the length of the country to the Andaman Sea. The river runs 1,370 miles (1,220km), fragmenting into the Ayeyarwady Delta for the last 250 miles (400km) or so; a place that offers a very different experience.

The Ayeyarwady starts out near the Tibetan border as two streams, the N'Mai and Mali. This is a rainy place and

the waters rush down through subtropical rainforest that is rich in rhododendrons. The river grows fast in the rain and for at least part of the year (monsoon season is generally May to October) is navigable to cruises from Myitkyina only 30 miles (50km) south of the streams' confluence. From here it flows through to romantic, colonial Mandalay, some 500 miles (800km) away, and on to Yangon (the modern name for Rangoon), almost double that.

The waters are wide, sometimes more than a mile across, but shallow, the scenery as undemanding as the river, flat with mountains rising in the distance. The river narrows as it heads south, making navigation difficult during the drier seasons, but cruises can leave year-round from Bhamo, a city where it dissolves into several muddy channels around grassy islands. This was an important trading post with China, only 30 miles (50km) away, until the 1800s, and still has sights such as the Chan Thar Ya Pagoda, which is golden and regal.

The Ayeyarwady bends to the west, meandering, wide and in many channels across vast plains where the domes of temples and Buddhist monasteries dot the torpid landscape. Yet on several occasions the river narrows, passing between cliffs up to 300ft (90m) high. Mostly, though, it is broad and serene, narrowing again only in the run up to Mandalay before becoming a mass of wandering channels as it reaches the city.

It's here that a number of classic Ayeyarwady cruises start, running the lengthy stretch down to Yangon, the latter actually on the Yangon river, which involves a 20-mile (32km) link on the Twante Canal.

Mandalay, the former royal capital is a big, bustling yet attractive place, the Royal Palace its heart, with temples dotting the lush surrounding plain.

A southern, riverside suburb is Amarapura (which at times usurped Mandalay as the country's capital), backing on to Taungthaman Lake, crossed by three-quarter-mile U-Bein Bridge, built in 1850, the world's oldest, longest teak bridge. Also teak is the iconic Bagaya Monastery. There are many more monasteries and temples to visit here and in Sagaing.

The riverside views are constantly changing, at times open and calm, at others a mass of rock towers and islands. As it reaches the volcanic Singu Plateau, the river makes a sharp right turn, then rolls across the plains eventually welcoming the Chindwin River from the west.

It's not quite all idyllic, the Ayeyarwady passes through

the industrial city of Yenangyaung before entering a peaceful valley with the Pegu Yoma Mountains to the east and the Arakan Mountains to the west.

Cruises call at places such as Bagan, with yet more teak monasteries, and distant views from Tan-Chi-Taung Mountain; Magwe, where the truly inspiring Myat-thalon Pagoda is built from solid gold bricks; Prome, surrounded by teak plantations: and Thayetmyo, a pleasing town that in the mid-19th century formed a sort of border between the British areas and the local folks.

The river then drifts into the delta. There are stretches that take commercial vessels but the cruise ships are mostly modern, shallow-draft vessels (with a contemporary colonial air), making it easy to navigate the often tortuous routes.

Arriving in Yangon is like arriving in Hollywood's idea of Asia, the bustle of the markets meeting the discreet elegance of European buildings, all the while with the Ayeyarwady sweeping through on its last leg to the sea.

The Ayeyarwady delta is, in effect, a giant paddy field. When the Brits were in charge here in the mid-19th century, the vast mix of wetland and jungle was cleared and cultivated, becoming somewhere that would feed the Raj.

Left: The U-Bein bridge, made of teak in 1850, stretches three-quarters of a mile(1.2km) across Taungthaman Lake

Above: The Ayeyarwady Delta is a sprawling area where the river becomes one with wetlands, dividing into many channels

Towns such as Bassein are still cloaked in colonial charm. The Ayeyarwady Flotilla Company (forerunner of leading Asian cruise line, Pandaw) by the 1920s, before roads, ran more than 100 steamers around the creeks and villages.

The river flows through seven main channels, from the Bassein River in the west to the Yangon River in the east, and a labyrinth of smaller ones. The scenery is a seemingly endless mix of water and grass-like greenery, dotted with temples and mosques between pretty villages.

Navigation depends on the season but cruises often take a circular route that involves Yangon on what passes for the main river, heading west to Bassein, a major port despite being 75 miles (120km) from the sea.

Big ships rise eerily from the flat surroundings as these have always been trading routes. Farther south the cultivated areas give way to coastal wildlife, where Mein Ma Hla Kyun Wildlife Reserve, a massive island mangrove swamp, is inhabited by saltwater crocodiles while thousands of birds swoop overhead.

THE BRAHMAPUTRA

Cruising with a backdrop of the Himalayas

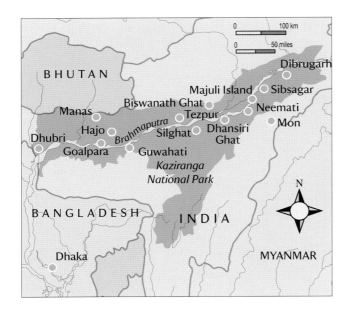

Above: Inside unassuming MV *Mahabaahu* is a world of fine cuisine, smart decor and a spa – as well as on-deck yoga

One of Asia's mightiest rivers, its journey starts as the Yarlung Tsangpo high in the Himalayas on the Angsi Glacier in Tibet (technically China these days, of course), flowing through a succession of great gorges before appearing in India's Assam Valley where it becomes the Brahmaputra. It eventually flows into the Ganges Delta in Bangladesh before reaching the Bay of Bengal.

It is the Indian stretch where river cruises operate, and it is an eye-opener, up to 20 miles (32km) wide, and that's in good weather; in monsoon season it can sprawl across the entire Assam plain. Back in colonial times the river hosted steamboat services but today it is more of a tourist route than a flowing highway.

The result is an expanse where you often see little but water and wildlife, dotted with the occasional community. Best not to forget that this is officially one of the wettest regions of the planet, so prepare for evocative mists. While every season can be rainy, the best time to explore is October to early April, which is when cruises operate.

Cruises are combined with safari excursions by boat, jeep and elephant and you can find yourself close to Indian tigers as well as the rare Greater One-horned Rhinoceros. Week-long cruises tend to sail between Guwahati and Majuli, some 220 miles (350km) away. The river is generally at least a couple of miles wide, a serene, shallow waterway, dotted with islands, rather than an open sea. River dolphins lazily splash, birds of prey hover over uninhabited islets and buffalo gaze from the banks with a hazy backdrop of the eastern Himalayas which top 24,000ft (7,300 metres).

The gentle, timeless journey takes in four national parks, passing terraced paddy fields and bright green tea plantations, Buddhist monasteries and Hindu schools. One of the leading ships is MV *Mahabaahu*, which has the unassuming aspect of a working vessel yet on board is a place of white tablecloths and discreet colonial trappings, even with swimming pool.

Guwahati, the largest city in north-east India, is backed by the foothills of the Shillong plateau. Sights include the hilltop Kamakhya Temple, a Hindu complex and an important place of pilgrimage with fantastical domed roofs created between the 8th and 17th centuries. The scenery constantly changes, from flatlands that seem to go on

Above: A simple ferry, a service offered for generations, is the only way to cross the river on long stretches where villages and farms are dotted

forever to tree-covered rock formations, both on the banks and emerging from the waters that loom up out of the mist. At Silghat a two-mile (3km) arched bridge, hypnotic in its simplicity, streaks across the river.

Kaziranga National Park, a UNESCO World Heritage Site, sprawling across the flood plains, is the place for a safari, plenty of rhinos as well as tigers, not to mention elephants, swamp deer and water buffalo.

Often a small craft takes passengers on a river safari where the River Dhansiri meets the Brahmaputra amongst tropical forest and towering elephant grass. Kingfishers dart, eagles soar and vultures hover while otters splash happily. There's often dinner on an island, served with all

the service and style of this dramatic country. There's also Majuli, the world's largest river island, home of the Mishing tribe, where river passengers get to experience dance, extravagant weaving and even more extravagant dress.

Many companies offer holidays involving MV *Mahabaahu*, some simply focusing on the cruise itself, others packaging it alongside a glorious tour of the Golden Triangle (Delhi, Agra, Jaipur) or with add-ons to spots such as Kolkata.

173

THE CHINDWIN
Colonial history with a cup of tea

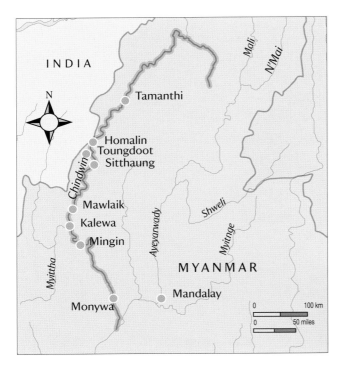

Right: RV *Zawgyi Pandaw*, one of a fleet of boutique ships, heads past countless temples on the Chindwin

bit farther down to the Ayeyarwady, then the 90 miles (145km) back up to Mandalay.

In the north the scenery is a sweep of lush forests and mountains, the land of tea and rubber plantations and the mellow fruitfulness of pineapple harvests. Cruise passengers, who make up most of the outsiders seen in this part of the world, are often entertained with songs, even war dances, by the Naga tribes who live in the hills.

Homalin, in its warm, wonderful setting, backed by the mountains and cosseted in a curve of the river, offers fabulous views from the peaceful, hilltop Buddha Lotus Garden while, a little farther down, remote Toungdoot even had a

This is the Ayeyarwady's greatest tributary, running a not inconsiderable distance through Myanmar (Burma) yet is a whole different prospect from its master. The northern part of the river is close to the Indian border and the Assam region, and is influenced by its neighbour.

Cruises tend to get as far as Homalin in the north, 200 miles (320km) west of the Ayeyarwady, and 400 miles (480km) upstream from where the rivers meet (although in the high-water season (June–November) small vessels can often get another 60 miles (100km), to Tamanthi, where the Tamanthi Wildlife Reserve is home to tigers, leopards, bears and elephants.

Itineraries often go as far as Monywa, a little to the south of Mandalay over on the Ayeyarwady; others go that little

hereditary ruler with palace and court in British times. To the south is Sitthaung, where in 1942 the advancing Japanese sank a number of Ayeyarwady Flotilla Company steamers; from here survivors of the invasion headed for the Indian border. Plans are already afoot to rescue and restore the ships' remains.

Mawlaik is a dreamy spot, settled by the Scottish-owned Bombay-Burma Trading Corporation in the 1920s – quaint timber bungalows sit on a delightful golf course and other British administrative buildings, even a post office, remain.

South of Mawlaik the river starts to twist and bend through the forests, the thick vegetation at times opening out to breathtaking mountain panoramas. Golden-tipped temples sit on tiny islands in the wide, muddy waters, sometimes backed by huge, rocky bluffs.

At Kalewa, on a snake-like wriggle of the river, the Myittha River joins from the west. Towards the south a landscape of rich farmland gradually drifts away and the river narrows to be surrounded by tree-lined hills. Here you come to Mingin, actually sitting on a several-mile loop of the river, a place rich in the teak monasteries, all ornately decorated, so prevalent in Myanmar.

A little farther and the Chindwin skirts Alaungdaw Kathapa National Park, which is filled with shrines and wildlife, where visitors can explore by truck, elephant, even dirt bike. The weather down here is less tropical, more a dry, savannah-like feel. Monywa is small city, home to the huge, colourful Thanboddhay Pagoda, dating from 1303, although rebuilt in 1939, with its sea of golden spires and treasure of more than half a million images of Buddha.

It's a grand place to finish – but you'll simply want to keep on going.

THE GANGES
Days of the Raj on the holy river

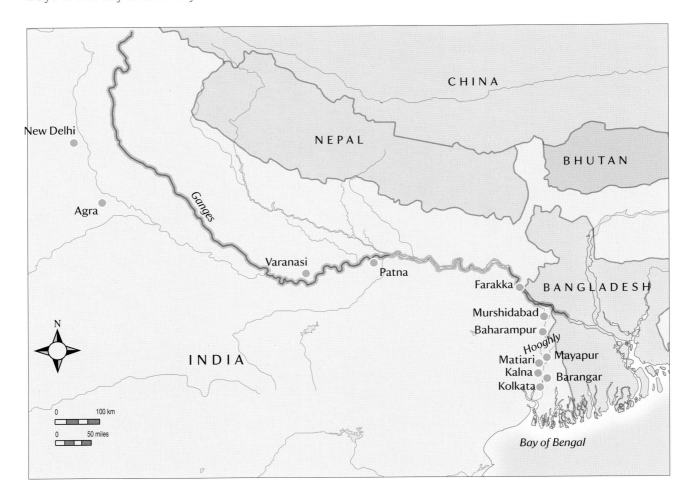

India's holy river dissects the country from the Himalayas on the Chinese border in the west across to Bangladesh in the east (where it becomes known as the Padma) before emptying into the Ganges Delta, where it is more a collection of rivers than one single waterway. The river is worshipped, providing a lifeline for the millions who live along its banks, despite the pollution that still sullies its waters.

The Ganges is a name that is often attributed to the region as a whole and many cruises are actually on one of the main river's spin-offs, the Hooghly, that drops south just before the Bangladesh border and passes through Kolkata before heading into the Bay of Bengal 250 miles

Right: The Victoria Memorial sits on the riverbank and is now a museum with artefacts from across the continents

(400km) east of the Padma (which by then is the Meghna).

The Hooghly, flowing 160 miles (260km) splits from the Ganges as a canal at the Farakka Barrage, where water is diverted to a power station and for drinking. Little, open boats act as ferries since bridges are few and far between. Cruise ships are discreet, often carrying fewer than 60 passengers in colonial style even though the vessels are very much 21st century.

Kolkata is a start point for a voyage upstream. The city itself is a picture postcard back to the days of the Raj, a place of grandiose buildings that retain their splendour to this day. The Victoria Memorial is a marble extravagance on the banks of the Hooghly, built between 1906 and 1921 and dedicated to Queen Victoria; it is now a museum and tourist attraction. See, too, Mother Teresa's former home, and her final resting place.

From the built-up city, the first stop is the town of Kalna with its Rajbari temple complex, an astonishing sight of 108 small, linked, marble Hindu temples, built early in the 19th century, sitting in twin circles in well-kept gardens. Many more temples rise up within view of the river.

The river twists and turns on itself, at one point a complete horseshoe taking an alternate route, with little islands and quiet channels. The scenery is a mix of fields

Below: The Temple of Bhukailash, one of 108 linked temples in the Rajbari complex alongside the river at Kalna, close to Kolkata

Right: The memorial to the battle of Plassey, on June 23, 1757, in which Clive of India cemented British rule for the next 200 years

and village life, never rushed, with the sound of a small, overloaded motorbike occasionally breaking the silence, an ox cart plodding by.

Mayapur, sitting between the Hooghly and Jalangi rivers, is the home of the Hare Krishna religious movement. Its headquarters are a complex of temples and gardens, topped by the new Temple of the Vedic Planetarium, an astonishing, ornate building with three blue-tiled domes, that is bigger than St Paul's Cathedral in London.

A little farther on the village of Matiari is a curiosity, a place of artisans who work brass and copper into intricate designs, who are, of course, willing to sell them to passing tourists who can also pop into the simple buildings to watch the making process.

Next comes Plassey, the site of the monumental battle that turned the history of both India and Britain. It was here, 95 miles (155km) north of Kolkata, on what are now grassy, peaceful banks, that in 1757 Clive of India defeated the Moghul Nawab, ruler of Bengal and his French allies, so setting things up for the East India Company to rule over

continent for almost two centuries. In less than 12 hours, 3,000 troops saw off a force of some 50,000 with its string of war elephants. The battle is marked at numerous memorials, statues and mausoleums including the Obelisks of Mir Madan.

The river passes through the city of Baharampur and a few miles after that is the town of Murshidabad, outwardly unassuming amongst hills. Yet this was the capital of Bengal before Kolkata was established. Here on a grassy sward running down to the river is one of the region's major sights, Hazarduari Palace, a place of Italian-style grandeur built in the early 19th century on the site of an ancient fort.

With its river views it's a pleasing place to stroll around and is now a museum with thousands of exhibits, from Indian royal relics to European paintings – and it supposedly has a thousand doors too. Nearby is the Katra mosque, a grand 18th-century design in tranquil gardens.

Other voyages are on small craft, 20 or so passengers, heading north-west from the Farakka Barrage, on the main channel of the Ganges for 250 miles (400km) to the city of Patna, a teeming place of two million people.

Just north of the barrage is the town of Rajmahal where Shah Jehan, who had the Taj Mahal built, spent his early years. With hills stretching away, this is an Indiana Jones landscape. Forts, mosques and other pieces of history are hidden in the forest.

The river continues to weave, disappearing behind islands and forming little channels and, in places – particularly Bhagalpur – narrowing and then swelling to lake-like proportions. The scenery is mostly fields stretching away into a hazy distance, dotted with a few hills. Near Bhagalpur is the Vikramshila Gangetic Dolphin Sanctuary, a 30-mile (50-km) stretch of river from Sultanganj to Kahalgaon, protecting the long-nosed mammal that mostly inhabits

the Ganges and the Brahmaputra and is now only a few hundred strong.

Unlike many rivers, the Ganges rarely feels like you're in the middle of nowhere. There are always small communities, farms and temples dotting the landscape. You may also see dolphins as you travel gently through time, and you can go on land for rickshaw rides, walks and visits to monasteries.

The Ganges heads much farther inland but isn't so open to cruise boats, even small ones, while the stretch of the Hooghly south of Kolkata is short and relatively without interest.

Below: The Italianate Hazarduari Palace is a treasure trove of everything from Indian artefacts to European art in a gorgeous riverside setting

THE KINABATANGAN

Wild wetlands and forests where the orangutans swing

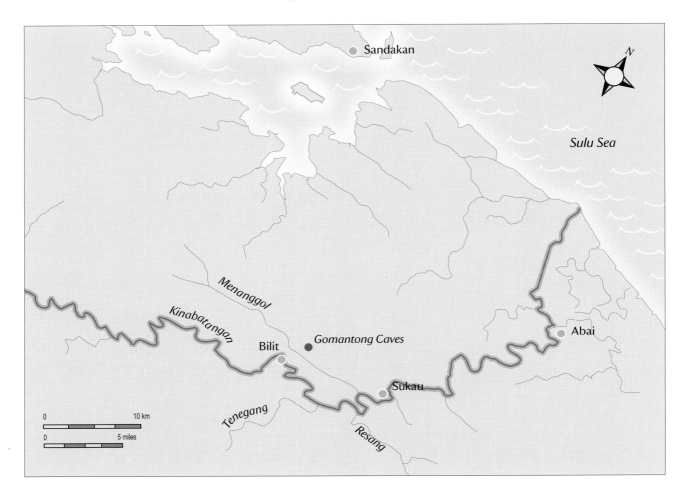

Deep in mysterious, romantic Malaysia, the Kinabatangan flows for 350 miles (560km) from the big, rugged mountains in the south-west to the Sulu Sea, east of the colonial city of Sandakan. The river is in Sabah, the east Malaysian state in the north of the island of Borneo.

This is a place of jungle with curiously shaped mountains dotting the horizon, where orangutans can be found in the forest canopy along with Proboscis Monkeys (brightly coloured with an extraordinary nose), while Asian Elephants (and even pygmy elephants) tramp through open areas and the mangrove swamps near the coast host Saltwater Crocodiles.

Watch out when the rains come. The monsoon, generally lasting between December and January, turns the coastal areas into a giant floodplain, reckoned to be Asia's biggest. This is unspoilt country where you'll see – and hear – wild cattle crashing through the undergrowth and maybe even see a leopard.

Cruises of several days can be found, mostly in the region closest to the coast. Here the river wanders in and out of numerous sections of the Kinabatangan Wildlife Sanctuary. The World Wildlife Fund oversees the Corridor of Life project that protects the river, aiming to create a balance between nature and the development, largely the

deforestation that has hit farther inland, for logging and for farming.

Boat trips often start from Sandakan, on the coast. Small, open craft operate on a daily basis (outnumbering the overnight cruises), often in conjunction with the riverside tourist lodges that sit in the middle of the wilderness. There are calls at places such as Abai Jungle Lodge, 30 miles (48km) upstream, only accessible by boat and having no running water or electricity. From here the river passes through the vast Lower Kinabatangan Segama Wetlands, a protected area of waterlogged forests, particularly Kulamba Wildlife Reserve, home to orangutans.

Sukau, a similar distance upstream from Abai, is little more than a collection of lodges, all with wooden walkways and accommodation on stilts to rise above the seasonal flooding. The scenery remains the same; the river, winding and not too wide, surrounded by dense jungle and the cacophony of tropical birds filling the air, the flash of brightly coloured feathers dotting the sky. Kingfishers skim the water while mighty Crested Serpent Eagles glide above. The little boats are able to negotiate small channels

Above left: Proboscis Monkeys offer a curious sight as they peer down from the lush canopy of the Bornean rainforests

Above: Asian Elephants, with their tiny ears, wallow in the cooling waters of the river, often in family groups

and take you to the very heart of the jungle, even if you didn't feel like you were in it before.

Another 40 miles (60km) or so and about 10 miles (15km) north of the river are Gomantong Caves, a winding cave system inside the limestone of Gomantong Hill with ceilings up to 180ft (60m) high. They are as big a tourist attraction as you can get in these parts: a colony of more than a quarter of a million Wrinkle-lipped Free-tailed Bats live here, swarming out each evening, entertaining the visitors from forest lodges.

The river goes on but this is pretty much it for tourists before the boats head back to the coast. Sandakan is the perfect place to finish. Head to the hilltop Puu Jih Shih Temple for stunning views across the sea, city – and of the river and jungle stretching away.

THE UPPER MEKONG
LAOS TO CHINA
A four-country cruise

The Mekong is a big river flowing 2,700 miles (4,350km) from the Tibetan Plateau through half a dozen nations, firstly China's Yunnan Province, then Myanmar, Thailand, Laos, Cambodia and Vietnam.

Yet despite its grand journey, its navigation is tortured due to falls, rapids and seasonal highs and lows. The biggest obstacle of all is just in Laos above the Cambodia border – the Khone Falls. The river becomes a turmoil of passages laced with rocks and islands. The falls have the nickname 'The 4,000 Islands' and in colonial times the French even built a railway around them to connect steamer services on the two stretches of the river.

In recent years the Pandaw cruise company has launched voyages from Laos all the way to China thanks to specially designed shallow draft ships with powerful engines.

The journey from Luang Prabang takes the best part of two weeks to Jinghong, a city founded in 1180 that has at times had Thai and Burmese occupations. Luang Prabang

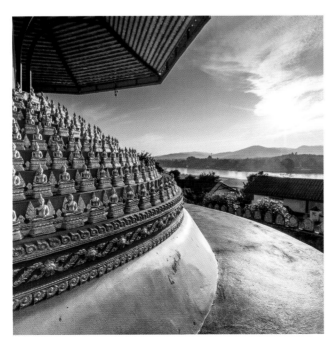

itself is a UNESCO World Heritage Site, filled with temples and surrounded by lush hills and mountains. The river, less than half a mile wide, is pure Asia – tree-covered banks rising from the muddy waters, palms fluttering in the breeze and the occasional beach with long, wooden canoes gliding by and children splashing.

An impressive call swiftly awaits: Pak Ou is a Buddhist sanctuary of two caves, dark and filled with religious icons, above the river in gigantic limestone cliffs where the Nam Ou river joins the Mekong.

The river, heading north, makes a great curve and heads east before sweeping north again, often rushing and narrow. In ever wilder surroundings the Mekong then forms the Laos-Thailand border for around 80 miles (130km). Nearby in Laos is the jungle of Nam Kan National Park where the Gibbon Experience allows visitors the chance to see the wildlife from high treehouses. Cruises call at tiny villages to visit markets and meet with local tribes.

Eventually there's a point where Laos, Thailand and Myanmar meet. Just before you get there the Golden Triangle Park both educates (try the Hall of Opium devoted to the drug's long history, as well as the varied temples) and challenges with forest walks and bicycle hire. At the triangle itself the infinitely wiggly Ruak river rushes down through the trees to join the Mekong, which then forms the Laos-Myanmar border for a good 150 miles (240km), a beguiling mix of beaches and forest. The river then becomes the China-Myanmar border before entering China itself (where it's called the Lancang river), a journey of 55 miles (90km) to Jinghong. This stretch is mainly through winding gorges, sometimes with steep sides, sometimes with lightly-forested hills, all having an unmistakably Oriental look. The river widens at Jinghong, with islands and varied channels – although the banks are often far from the waters in the dry season in the early part of the year. Ancient meets modern as an historic, pagoda-rich roofscape gives way to the Sipsongpanna suspension bridge, with small river cruise ships gliding back and forth.

Far left: The river panorama from one of the many hillside temples in Luang Prabang

Left: Tributes to Buddha line the river, often placed in high, out-of-the-way spots

THE LOWER MEKONG
VIETNAM TO CAMBODIA
Cities, floating markets and some of the world's greatest temples

Right: Cruise ships on the Mekong, such as Pandaw's RV *Mekong*, are traditional looking but offer a luxury lifestyle

Mention the Mekong and people think Vietnam, even though the river flows all the way from China through six countries. But it is the southernmost stretch where most of the action is.

Once the river enters Cambodia it has pretty much had its fill from tributaries pouring down from the mountains and the river is a placid, dreamy affair as it passes through flat, open countryside.

During the Vietnam War, the west bank was a battlefield as attacks took place on communist forces in Laos but now the region is at peace, an entrancing mix of paddy fields set against jungle-covered hills, shimmering, golden

Buddhist temples and bustling markets — some of them floating on the river's muddy waters.

River cruises here are many, with a clutch of leading international companies offering voyages on small, modern ships built in traditional style, full of gleaming wood and colonial airs and graces. Most sail from near the colonial charm of Ho Chi Minh City (still known by many as Saigon, and with boat excursions on its Saigon river) up through the Vietnamese heartland and into Cambodia but where they get to depends on the ship as the river is seasonally deprived of water. Some follow the Mekong as far as the French colonial town of Kratie. Almost all river

cruises take the fork, at the town of Phnom Penh, up the Tonle Sap River, perhaps as far as the village of Kampong Trolach. Many then take a coach to Siem Reap and the huge temple complex of Angkor. Some, though, on ships with very shallow draft, continue the length of 80-mile (130-km) Tonlé Sap, a freshwater lake, to within 10 miles (16km) of Siem Reap.

At its southern end the Mekong enters the South China Sea in three main channels anything up to a mile wide and up to 20 miles (24km) apart. It's a delta filled with islands, where beach resorts sit side by side with bird sanctuaries, lush greenery giving way to well-irrigated farmland.

Cruises mostly set off from My Tho, a small city dating from the 17th century when it was a huge commercial hub for the river and Ho Chi Minh City. Now it is a tourist hub with sights such as the ornate, 19th-century Vĩnh Tràng temple and floating markets.

The Mekong gradually brings together its various strands but it is 40 miles (65km) before it becomes a single river. At the final meeting is Vĩnh Long, a small city that cruise passengers often visit on a sampan tour to see how local products such as rice paper, rice wine and even sampans are made. From here the river heads north-west into Vietnam's interior, a 90-mile (145-km) journey to the

Cambodian border through misty, ageless scenery, the river up to a mile wide.

Cruises call at Tân Châu, just before the border, where the river is flat and wide. Standalone Sam Mountain rises just outside town, reached by a sampan ride through the backwaters. The mountain gives an overview of river, plains and the peaks that rise across the river.

Phnom Penh is 70 miles (110km) away along a largely featureless stretch of wide river, enlivened by the soaring 2015 Neak Loeung suspension bridge, a huge contrast to the ramshackle town of the same name that its illuminated spans cast in a golden glow at night.

Phnom Penh is a beacon of civilisation in the midst of a country that seems to be from another century, where ox carts trundle along the riverside roads, and both men and women of indeterminate age perform backbreaking work in the paddy fields. The Cambodian capital is a bastion of French colonial grandeur and you sail in past the domes of the Royal Palace as smartly dressed folk stroll along the

Above: Tonlé Sap should be on everyone's bucket list but only ships with a shallow draft can make it through

Below: Neuk Loeung bridge shines like a beacon over a rural stretch of river far from the bright lights of Phnom Penh

Corniche, the tree-lined riverside path rich with bars and restaurants. There are markets and monasteries, beaches and bridges. Yet for all the fun (riding in three-wheeled bicycle taxis) there's a serious side, with the Tuol Sleng Genocide Museum, a former school where 17,000 prisoners of the Khmer Rouge were held, and the barbarous Killing Fields. Outside the Royal Palace, the Mekong heads north-east while the Tonle goes north-west.

The river quickly becomes less open to larger vessels, as it darts around islands and forms varied channels. It passes the 8th-century hilltop Wat Hanchey temple on the 80-mile (130-km) journey to Kampong Cham, which is alive with more colonial buildings. Here a long, wobbly bamboo bridge crosses the Mekong's narrower strand to the park-like Koh Pen Island with its palms and big beaches.

This is pretty much the limit for most cruises although the Pandaw cruise company's specially built MV *Tonle Pandaw* is able to head up as far as Kratie, another colonial town, where the whale-like Irrawaddy Dolphin is found.

Above: The ornate Royal Palace is one of the wonders of Phnom Penh, ancient creations sitting alongside colonial splendour

Below: RV *Mekong Navigator*, part of the luxury Uniworld fleet, offers French colonial style in boutique surroundings

THE RED RIVER
From jungle to the colonial wonder of Hanoi

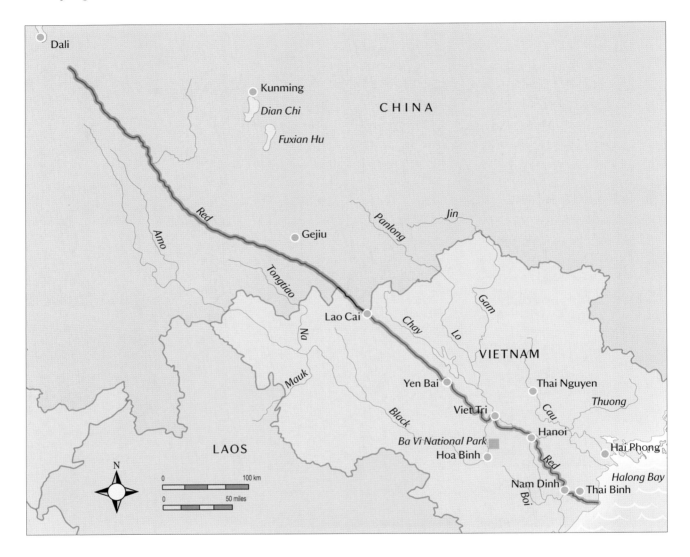

Right: The Red River is a journey through history as it cuts through Vietnam from top to bottom, emerging in the Gulf of Tonkin

It's red for a reason. Thanks to a combination of the rich, reddish-brown earth and waters that are given to wild seasonal floods, the river is muddy but bright. The Red River, some 700 miles (1,110km) long, originates in Yunnan in south-west China and runs the length of Vietnam, through the capital, Hanoi, into the Gulf of Tonkin. The mouth is at Xuan Thuy National Park, all mangrove swamps and wetlands, where rare Chinese white dolphins and finless porpoises can often be seen. And yet villages for miles

around sit on the Red River Delta, a fertile expanse criss-crossed by rivers, some sizeable and navigable, many not.

Red River cruises (scarce compared to those on Vietnam's Mekong) tend to start 50 miles (80km) east of the river's mouth, in Halong Bay, a place seen in many photos and which looks like the prehistoric setting for a movie. Jagged limestone rocks and craggy islands, 1,600 of them, covered in mini rainforests, jut from the emerald waters. Junks potter about, kayakers pedal quietly.

Cruises take varied paths, often depending on weather and water levels but most zig-zag across towards Hanoi. The Thái Bình is one route, although it's often difficult to know just where you are as the small, shallow boats make their way through jungle with calls at villages for food tastings, water puppet shows and dance. The small but bustling city of Thái Bình itself is 30 miles (48km) south of the River Thái Bình, on the Sông Trà Lý.

The Red River is reached about halfway between coast and Hanoi. The town is a mix of casual Asian life – the food shacks, the mopeds – and graceful French colonial architecture. The river is crossed by a number of bridges, not least chunky New York-like Long Bien Bridge completed in 1899. The River Duong joins here and a lengthy promontory between the two is full of markets and tiny streets.

Head north-east and the throng of the city gives way to an older world. There are endless paddy fields and more limestone crags creating a mystical, timeless atmosphere. The river sweeps into lake-like bends, then narrows for straighter stretches, sometimes splitting into two channels.

Another 45 miles (70km) further is the industrial city of Viet Tri, on a big, island-filled bend, where the Song Lo joins from the north, curling around the back of the city. Just before the rivers meet there's the ancient village of Duong Lam, where temples and pagodas mix with the simple brick architecture of agricultural workers.

Sail up the Song Lo and you're heading for the wilds, the mountains looming in the distance towards China. Cruises often visit villages up here, then turn about, round the city bend and journey down the Da River. Mountains rear up and you reach Ba Vì National Park, a place of waterfalls and little temples amongst tropical forest, mists drifting down from the heights. It's about as far as cruises go before negotiating the jungle back to the coast.

THE YANGTZE

Gorges, dams and a nation from end to end

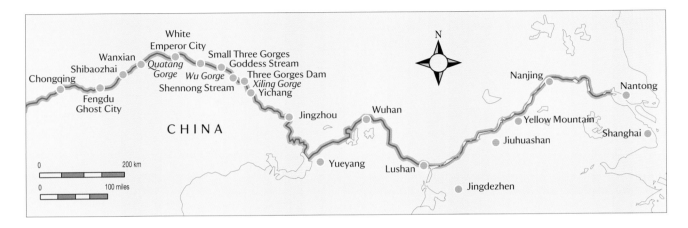

Gliding down the serene Yangtze, the huge, vertical canyon walls reaching for the sky, you know that you can't be anywhere but China. Little trees froth out from the rocks, and every so often there's a colourful pagoda outlined against the sky.

There's something about the light, the haze as the layers of rock stretching into the distance turn purple in the fading sun. In other places, paddy fields stretch for miles and farmland is tended as it has been for centuries, fruitful in the sub-tropical temperatures that cloak much of the Yangtze which goes almost from one side of the country to the other.

This is a special river, and not just for the statistics. Although the facts that at a little over 3,900 miles (6,300km) it's the third longest river in the world (after the Amazon and Nile), the longest river in Asia and the longest in the world to remain in one country do much to impress. It's simply that it's so different, so ancient, including the highlight, the Three Gorges, one of the world's great

Left: The spirit of China, an ornate pagoda reaching for the sky as the relentless Yangtze flows calmly on into the distance

Above: The Three Gorges, which stretch for miles with rocky bluffs, often covered with delicate trees, towering above the river

natural wonders – until you come to the Three Gorges Dam, with its five-stage lock, the world's biggest.

Although there are varied opinions, the river is generally agreed to originate from a collection of headwaters, some more than 17,000ft (5,200m) up on the Tibetan Plateau. It wanders through deep valleys amid the mountains, dropping pretty much down to sea level in the first 1,600 miles (2,600km).

Yet despite its length, river cruises tend to be no more than a few days long, getting no further upstream than Chongqing and down as far as Yichang or Wuhan, but not, mostly, to the East China Sea where you'll find the splendid colonial city of Shanghai.

Chongqing is a sprawling city of 30 million people in a region of forests and mountains. The zoo here is as good as

Top: The huge locks of the Three Gorges Dam can take a day to negotiate but have become a tourist attraction in themselves

Above: One of the mighty monuments at Fengdu Ghost City, gazing down from the heights of Ming Mountain

zoos get, and what China is all about, with giant pandas as well as the fluffy, cat-like red panda, the South China tiger and exquisite white tiger.

On the first stretch east of Chongqing is Fengdu. The city sits on the south bank but across the wide river, on Ming Mountain, is Fengdu Ghost City, a wonderful complex of shrines, temples and monasteries dedicated to China's devotion to the afterlife.

The Three Gorges start farther east from here and continue for 190 miles (305km) to Yichang. This is a stretch of breathless beauty, limestone walls, mountains peeking over the top, and the waters passing relentlessly through. First is Qutang Gorge, the shortest, narrowest and most spectacular of the three, featuring tree-covered walls closing in on both sides. Here, not far from Fengdu, and a call on many cruises, is Shibaozhai, where an extraordinary 12-storey red pagoda, dating back to 1650, provides a stairway from the lush riverside hill to the temple at the top of a rocky outcrop.

Wu Gorge stretches for 30 miles (50km), offering a primitive landscape, narrow with near vertical walls reaching 2,000ft (600m) in parts. Travellers are often transferred to a sampan for a ride along the Goddess Stream, an ultra-narrow gorge that runs for 10 miles (16km), from which it is often difficult to see the sky amidst the lush trees and flowers.

Another small-boat additional adventure is to the Lesser Three Gorges on the Daning River, one of the Yangtze's main tributaries, extending for more than 30 miles (50km). Here there are waterfalls and the entrances to even smaller gorges, not least Longmen Gorge with its Ancient Plank Road high on the cliffs.

Xiling Gorge is the longest and perfect for sitting back on deck and enjoying the view. The flow is interrupted by the dam and the locks, which provide a lengthy yet no less relaxing diversion, and there are tours that let you see the dam up close, exploring what is the world's largest hydro-electric power station.

The views have changed in many places since the Three Gorges Dam was completed in 2012 thanks to rising water levels all the way back to Chongqing but the result is still spectacular, just different, with so many towns and antiquities sadly lost beneath the surface.

Yichang is where the gorges come to an end, only 25 miles (40km) downstream from the dam but presenting a different face to the world, sitting on a wide river bend, with modern buildings gleaming in the twilight and a haze covering the peaks across the river while little boats potter about as they have done for so many centuries. The mouth of the gorge is like a giant's gateway, houses climbing the tree-covered slopes and the great arch of a dizzying bridge way above.

Farther along, the city of Jingzhou dares people to invade. Along the river the ancient city walls rise 30ft (9m), and they are wider than they are tall, watchtowers rising

Above right: Shibaozhai's 12-storey pagoda that is actually a hidden staircase providing access to the temple

Right: Zhonghua Gate, dating from the 14th century, part of the city wall in Nanjing, China's capital during the Ming Dynasty

even higher. The Yangtze at one point is well over a mile wide with great sandbank islands looking like secret hide-aways in the middle.

At Shishou the river does a U-turn, creating Dongting Lake as it does so while at Yueyang two even bigger lakes spring out on a bend. A little farther on, vast Honghu Lake, known for its display of lotus flowers, sits a couple of miles from the river, connected by canal.

Vast lakes now start to spread out across the country-side. By the time you get to Wuhan, the gorges are left behind and the city is almost as much water as it is land. There are lakes and waterways everywhere. Wuhan is a big city, one that was important in the Chinese Revolution; the 1911 Wuchang Uprising led to the end of the Qing dynasty and the start of the Republic of China. There are modern towers and even beach resorts on the lakes. It is here also that you find the First Yangtze River Bridge, a road and rail affair that, amazingly, was only completed in 1957 when it was the most easterly crossing point.

Most internationally marketed cruises end or start here, often packaged with a much bigger, land-based itinerary, taking in Beijing, Xian (for the Terracotta Warriors) and Shanghai.

The most scenic part of the river is behind you but some companies do offer cruises all the way to Shanghai, adding another couple of days to the trip. A little farther on, still amongst the lakes, is Huanggang, another big city, with the Dabie Mountains rising as a backdrop to the north. The big attraction is the city's namesake, Mount Huangshan, a UNESCO World Heritage Site, known as 'the loveliest mountain of China'.

The mass of knobbly granite peaks, often climbing to well over 3,000ft (1,000m) high and so often seen poking through misty clouds, has been a major inspiration in Chinese art, finding its way into everything from paintings to dinner plates. A trip up here gives magnificent views

Left: The ornate Jing'an Temple in Shanghai, first built in 247AD, stands proudly next to one of the thriving city's contemporary glass giants

amid otherworldly scenery of gnarled trees and strangely shaped rocks.

The lakes continue to follow the mile-wide river. At Jiuijang, between lake and river, is Mount Lushan National Park, another UNESCO-protected scenic wonder. The mountain itself is an oval peak with its head in the clouds, reaching nearly 5,000ft (1,500m).

The park is a place of lakes, hot springs, caverns, temples and gardens. As the Yangtze leaves it passes either side of a huge isle of farmland and, over the next 100 miles (160km) constantly divides into varied channels. Big towns pass by with Nanjing the next major city, still almost 200 miles (320km) from Shanghai.

This was the country's capital for a time in the Ming dynasty and there's a wealth of history, including the Zhonghua Gate, part of the 14th-century city wall. Here, in a park, is the mausoleum of Dr Sun Yat-sen, founding father of the Republic of China.

From here the journey to Shanghai is straightforward, with the wonders of the river fighting with the wonders of the soaring buildings for attention. It's here that the river cruise ships meet the ships of the ocean plus all the little boats that offer trips around the harbour. By the time the river gets here it's more than five miles (8km) across, divided by various islands.

The Huangpu is the Yangtze's last major tributary, a 70-mile (112km) man-made creation, dug more than 200 years BC on the orders of Lord Chunshen, one of the Four Lords of the Warring States. It flows through the heart of Shanghai, past colonial mansions as well as gleaming sky-scrapers such as the futuristic Shanghai World Financial Center. Cruises along here are plentiful and nighttime cruises, with Chinese cuisine for dinner, are also popular. The river is peaceful in a teeming city, as popular with locals as with visitors.

Shanghai might be as far as the Yangtze goes but there's plenty of water-bound entertainment still to enjoy in a city that combines both the history and the future of China. Thanks to the islands this is a city of ferries and has been for a century or more - almost 20 ferry lines serve almost 40 stops and cost very little for a foot passenger.

Rocky bluffs provide a stunning
backdrop to the Murray River

Australia
& New Zealand

THE MURRAY

A voyage through the outback, and you may even spot a koala

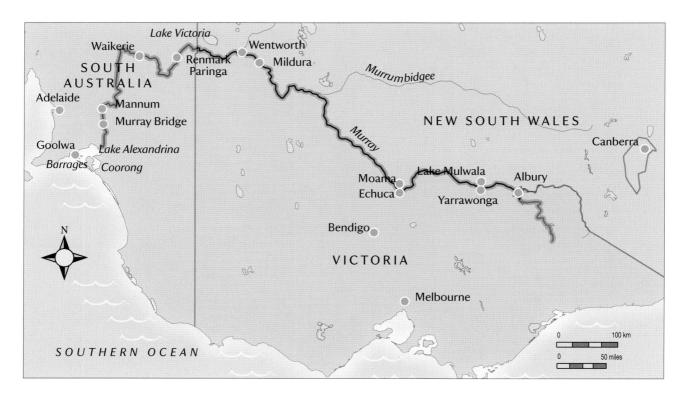

The true spirit of Australia and its longest river at 1,560 miles (2,500km), the Murray River cuts across the country from east to west. Travel it in one go and you will see mountains and outback, desert and gum tree forest, everything that you think of when you think of Australia. Yet the Murray is shallow, often narrow and prone to drought so only small river cruise vessels can negotiate it.

It rises in the Australian Alps, to the north-east of Melbourne, then wanders north-west across the plains, hugging the border between New South Wales and Victoria before flowing into South Australia. There's a sharp turn south as it heads for the ocean just south of Adelaide – but doesn't quite make it, ending in 25-mile (40km) Lake Alexandrina behind its picturesque barrier islands, which puts paid to any proper shipping traffic.

River cruises, both sightseeing and up to seven days long, on a number of small vessels, operate on the stretch

Right: *Spirit of the Murray* is dwarfed by the limestone cliffs, some of the river's tallest, near Lake Alexandrina

nearest the ocean, many based at the town of Murray Bridge (site of the river's first bridge in 1869), not too far from Adelaide. Even here the varied scenery is apparent, whether it is sunny-hued limestone cliffs or bleakly beautiful scrubland, well-tended farms or the neat surrounds of holiday cottages.

Pelicans swoop for fish and cockatoos sit in the trees; at night owls break the big silence with their calls. And you really are likely to see Koalas, kangaroos and Emus, either as you glide along the slow-flowing river or as you take hikes into the back country.

Yet it is possible to explore the river to the full. PS *Murray Princess*, the biggest working paddlewheeler in this part of

the world, and thoroughly traditional looking, operates week-long cruises with onboard accommodation. The small, modern boats of Spirit of Australia (the only company to sail the entire river) cruise varied stretches with up to eight days' sailing and nights in hotels, between Goolwa, amid the islands on the edge of Lake Alexandrina, the biggest freshwater lake in Australia, and Albury on the edge of the mountains.

Paddlesteamers are part of the river's history with more than 100 plying its waters during the late 19th century, delivering supplies and helping move farm produce of grain and wool. Many boats today may be more modern yet they continue to celebrate the river's heritage travelling one of the world's longest rivers yet one that is small and safe.

The Aboriginal history of the region, dating back more than 40,000 years, is apparent and local tribes regale travellers with tales of the river. Ngaut Ngaut Conservation Park, atop the cliffs, is one of the country's leading Aboriginal archaeological sites.

From Goolwa, cruises cross Lake Alexandrina then gently pass riverbanks lined with dairy farms and those golden cliffs (this stretch has the river's highest cliffs). Stops tend to include the historic customs house at the New South Wales-Victoria border and a visit to Banrock Station winery as you pass through the fertile Riverland, famed for its vineyards, and almond and citrus orchards. At the tiny town of Paringa, where the river is lined with willow trees, boats pass under the 1927 lift bridge.

Some trips take a sidestep to travel up the Darling River in the flatlands just before Mildura, itself all but surrounded by lakes including billabongs (oxbow lakes).

After Mildura the river heads south-east, passing through Kemendok National Park, a place for camping and

walking on beaches, and Kemendok Nature Reserve, the levees and flood plains rich in red gum trees and swamp. There's no logic to the river's course, as it snakes and doubles back, wiggling wherever it decides.

The next major town is Echuca, once Australia's largest inland port, and the closest point on the river to Melbourne. The name Echuca is Aboriginal for 'Meeting of the Waters' – the Murray is here joined by the Campaspe. This is also the borderlands, the town in Victoria but Moama on the northern side of the Murray is in New South Wales.

This is where paddlesteamers flourished in the 1800s (more than 100 were built in Echuca) and it is now home to the world's largest collection of the vessels. Echuca Wharf, what's left of Red Gum Wharf, which stretched a quarter of a mile, is now a history centre. Echuca Paddlesteamers offers trips on historic paddlesteamers, PS *Pevensey*, built in 1911, and PS *Alexander Arbuthnot* (1923), with occasional outings on PS *Adelaide*, built in 1866 and the oldest wooden-hulled paddlesteamer working in the world.

Murray River Paddlesteamers, offers cruises on PS *Emmylou*, claiming to be the only wood-fired paddlesteamer (fuelled by red gum logs) in the world offering regular overnight cruising (up to four nights).

Paradoxically, water levels on the river around here can be at their best during the hot Australian summer (November–December) thanks to irrigation waters from Hume Dam, just the other side of the town of Albury.

Heading farther upstream the feeling of isolation grows even stronger as what little traffic there is gets even thinner. Only the smallest craft can operate here amongst the currents and shallows. Here is Barmah National Park, with Ulupna Island, part of one of the country's largest red gum forests. The narrow river expands into 15-mile (24km) Lake Mulwala set amongst various protected parklands.

The end of the line is Albury, just before the river emerges into Lake Huma at the bottom of the mountains. Monument Hill is the place for views of the river disappearing into the distance.

Left: PS *Emmylou*, fired by red gum logs, offers cruises that last for several days in the hypnotising scenery near the town of Echuca

THE WHANGANUI

Volcanoes tower over primordial island scenery

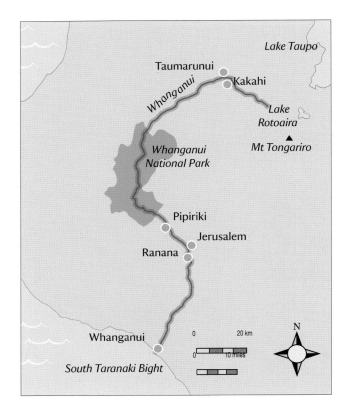

The fresh, clear beauty of New Zealand is encapsulated in the Whanganui. The river runs only 180 miles (290km) from mountain to ocean on North Island yet is a picture of beauty from end to end.

For much of its upper reaches it is encompassed by Whanganui National Park, a place of wild, untouched scenery — gorges, bluffs and a forest canopy alive with birdlife. It rises on the northern slopes of Mount Tongariro, one of three active volcanoes that dot the region, near Lake Rotoaira. There are views as far as snow-tipped Mount Taranaki, 50 miles (80km) away.

The river first flows north before a short south turn taking it through seemingly endless hilly valleys, visiting little towns including Pipiriki and Jerusalem, the latter with palm trees alongside denser greenery, to the Tasman Sea at the city of Whanganui itself. While only the country's third longest river, it is nevertheless the longest navigable one despite rarely being wide and often dotted with rapids.

As far back as 1892 it was possible to take a Thomas Cook trip on paddlesteamer PS *Waimarie*, exploring 'The Rhine of Maoriland' from Whanganui up to little Pipiriki, 50 miles (80km) from the coast amongst the lush hills of the river valley. A paddlesteamer passenger service ran as late as 1958.

Waimarie spent 50 years at the bottom of the river but was relaunched in 2000, still coal-fired. She now sails from the Waimarie Centre and Museum, a restored 19th-century sailing club, in Whanganui, offering two-hour cruises amid the cliffs and home-covered hillsides of the early stages of the river.

Another historic boat, MV *Wairua*, sails from Whanganui's Moutoa Gardens, once a Maori habitat, on a sharp bend in the river. The vessel, built in London, started sailing here in 1904, a pioneer of river travel above Pipiriki thanks to its then-revolutionary, tunnel-drive system, a forerunner of today's jet boats. Cruises see the city give way to bush-covered countryside, farmland and rolling hills, some heading for Hipango Park, a large area of bush reached only by river, full of walks and wild birds.

Only the paddleboat *Adventurer II* makes the full 140-mile (230-km) trip up to Taumarunui, even then only during times of high water, forced to cut the journey short at other times of the year. Here the Whanganui is narrow and fast, curving amongst the verdant hills with the air of an energetic country river. Indeed, there are rapids farther downstream, and rafts and canoes are far from an unusual sight. The four-day trip (with hotel accommodation) on a re-creation of an historic, flat-bottomed steamer involves stretches where the boat has to be winched or poled over difficult sections.

From just north of Pipiriki, Bridge To Nowhere operates jet-boat tours that take you roaring through primordial scenery — untouched lush greenery cloaking the banks,

which disappear into deep gorges where caves, ferns and rapids give a science-fiction adventure feel in a section of the river that riverboats used to fight to negotiate more than a century ago. Walks head to (and over) the Bridge To Nowhere, a grand, arching road crossing of the Mangapurua Stream tributary in Whanganui National Park. Once used to transport goods it is now reached only by hikers passing silently through the primordial scenery.

Above: The river passes through the lush, dramatic setting of Whanganui National Park, surrounded by volcanoes

Right: The Bridge To Nowhere is part of a hiking trail on a former road, crossing Mangapurua Stream, a Whanganui tributary

WHO GOES WHERE

The world's rivers are served by a wide range of companies, from those offering boutique luxury in cutting-edge ships to those serving up adventure in an historic vessel. Either way, a river journey is an extraordinary experience. Here are companies offering voyages around the globe.

EUROPE

Amsterdam's Waterways
amawaterways.co.uk; avaloncruises.co.uk; croisieurope.co.uk; europeanwaterways.com; scenic.co.uk; noble-caledonia.co.uk; rivieratravel.co.uk; saga.co.uk; shearings.com; uniworld.com; vikingrivercruises.co.uk

Caledonian Canal
caledonian-discovery.co.uk; europeanwaterways.com; leboat.co.uk; lordoftheglens.co.uk; themajesticline.co.uk;

Danube
amawaterways.co.uk; aptouring.co.uk; avaloncruises.co.uk; croisieurope.co.uk; crystalcruises.co.uk; emeraldwaterways.co.uk; fredolsencruises.com; noble-caledonia.co.uk; rivieratravel.co.uk; saga.co.uk; scenic.co.uk; shearings.com; tauck.co.uk; titantravel.co.uk; uniworld.com; vikingrivercruises.co.uk

Dnieper
noble-caledonia.co.uk; vikingrivercruises.co.uk

Douro
amawaterways.co.uk; aptouring.co.uk; avaloncruises.co.uk; croisieurope.co.uk; emeraldwaterways.co.uk; scenic.co.uk; noble-caledonia.co.uk; rivieratravel.co.uk; saga.co.uk; shearings.com; titantravel.co.uk; uniworld.com; vikingrivercruises.co.uk; europarques.com; leyendadelpisuerga.com

Elbe
croisieurope.co.uk; cruiseandmaritime.com; cunard.co.uk; fredolsencruises.com; noble-caledonia.co.uk; pocruises.com; saga.co.uk; vikingrivercruises.co.uk

Gironde-Dordogne
amawaterways.co.uk; aptouring.co.uk; croisieurope.co.uk; french-waterways.com; scenic.co.uk; noble-caledonia.co.uk; uniworld.com; vikingrivercruises.co.uk; voyagestoantiquity.com

Gironde-Garonne
amawaterways.co.uk; europeanwaterways.com; noble-caledonia.co.uk; uniworld.com; vikingrivercruises.co.uk

Guadalquivir
croisieurope.co.uk; crucerosensevilla.com; fredolsencruises.com; guadaluxe.com; saga.co.uk; voyagestoantiquity.com

Main
amawaterways.co.uk; aptouring.co.uk; avaloncruises.co.uk; croisieurope.co.uk; crystalcruises.co.uk; emeraldwaterways.co.uk; fredolsencruises.com; noble-caledonia.co.uk; rivieratravel.co.uk; scenic.co.uk; shearings.com; tauck.co.uk; uniworld.com

Marne
belmond.com; croisieurope.co.uk; europeanwaterways.com

Moselle
amawaterways.co.uk; avaloncruises.co.uk; croisieurope.co.uk; crystalcruises.co.uk; emeraldwaterways.co.uk; fredolsencruises.com; noble-caledonia.co.uk; rivieratravel.co.uk; saga.co.uk; scenic.co.uk; shearings.com; tauck.co.uk; uniworld.com

Po
croisieurope.co.uk; europeanwaterways.com; leboat.co.uk; saga.co.uk; titantravel.co.uk; uniworld.com

Rhine
amawaterways.co.uk; aptouring.co.uk; avaloncruises.co.uk; croisieurope.co.uk; crystalcruises.co.uk; emeraldwaterways.co.uk; fredolsencruises.com; noble-caledonia.co.uk; rivieratravel.co.uk; saga.co.uk; scenic.co.uk; shearings.com; tauck.co.uk; titantravel.co.uk; uniworld.com; vikingrivercruises.co.uk

Rhone and Saône
aptouring.co.uk; avaloncruises.co.uk; belmond.com; croisieurope.co.uk; emeraldwaterways.co.uk; noble-caledonia.co.uk; rivieratravel.co.uk; scenic.co.uk; tauck.co.uk; uniworld.com; vikingrivercruises.co.uk

Sava
croisieurope.co.uk; regina-rivercruises.com

Seine
amawaterways.co.uk; avaloncruises.co.uk; croisieurope.co.uk; cruiseandmaritime.com; fredolsencruises.com; scenic.co.uk; rivieratravel.co.uk; shearings.com; tauck.co.uk; uniworld.com; vikingrivercruises.co.uk

Shannon
leboat.co.uk; europeanwaterways.com

Thames
african-queen.co.uk; citycruises.com; cruiseandmaritime.com; europeanwaterways.com; leboat.co.uk; salterssteamers.co.uk; thamesclippers.com; turks.co.uk

Tisza
croisieurope.co.uk

Volga-Svir
aptouring.co.uk; croisieurope.co.uk; emeraldwaterways.co.uk; noble-caledonia.co.uk; saga.co.uk; scenic.co.uk; titantravel.co.uk; uniworld.com; vikingrivercruises.co.uk; volgadream.com

NORTH AMERICA

Columbia
americancruiselines.com; americanqueensteamboatcompany.com; lightbluetravel.co.uk

Hudson
americancruiselines.com; circleline42.com; hudsonrivercruises.com; spiritcruises.com

Illinois
americanqueensteamboatcompany.com; lightbluetravel.co.uk; wendellaboats.com

Mississippi
americancruiselines.com; americanqueensteamboatcompany.com; lightbluetravel.co.uk; noble-caledonia.co.uk

St Johns
americancruiselines.com; sjrivercruises.com; stjohnsrivershipco.com

St Lawrence
blountsmallshipadventures.com; croisieurope.co.uk; cruiseandmaritime.com; crystalcruises.co.uk; ponant.com

Yukon
yukonrivercruises.com; klondikespirit.com

SOUTH AMERICA

Amazon
avaloncruises.co.uk; croisieurope.co.uk; cruiseandmaritime.com; cunard.co.uk; fredolsencruises.com; gadventures.co.uk; noble-caledonia.co.uk; ponant.com

Orinoco
journeylatinamerica.co.uk; ponant.com

AFRICA

Chobe
amawaterways.co.uk; croisieurope.co.uk; zqcollection.com

Congo
congotravelandtours.com; elmundosafaris.com

Niger
nigertravelandtours.com; sagatours.com

Nile
aggressor.com; noble-caledonia.co.uk; nourelnil.com; rivieratravel.co.uk; scenic.co.uk; uniworld.com; vikingrivercruises.co.uk

Senegal
bouelmogdad.com

Zambezi
croisieurope.co.uk; karibahouseboats.com

ASIA

Brahmaputra
mahabaahucruiseindia.com; noble-caledonia.co.uk

Ganges
aptouring.co.uk; avaloncruises.co.uk; gadventures.co.uk; pandaw.com; rivieratravel.co.uk; uniworld.com

Ayeyarwady
aptouring.co.uk; avaloncruises.co.uk; belmond.com; croisieurope.co.uk; emeraldwaterways.co.uk; noble-caledonia.co.uk; pandaw.com; scenic.co.uk; vikingrivercruises.co.uk

Chindwin
pandaw.com

Kinabatangan
borneodream.com

Mekong
amawaterways.co.uk; aptouring.co.uk; avaloncruises.co.uk; croisieurope.co.uk; emeraldwaterways.co.uk; gadventures.co.uk; noble-caledonia.co.uk; pandaw.com; rivieratravel.co.uk; scenic.co.uk; uniworld.com; vikingrivercruises.co.uk

Red
pandaw.com

Yangtze
aptouring.co.uk; croisieurope.co.uk; rivieratravel.co.uk; uniworld.com; tauck.co.uk; victoriacruises.com; vikingrivercruises.co.uk

AUSTRALIA & NEW ZEALAND

Murray
echucapaddlesteamers.net.au; murrayprincess.com.au; spiritaustraliacruises.com.au

Whanganui
canoesafaris.co.nz; waimarie.co.nz; whanganuiriver.co.nz; whanganuiriverboat.co.nz

INDEX

Abai 181
Abingdon 89
Abu Simbel 156
  Queen Nefertari Temple 156
  Ramesses II Temple 156
Abydos 159
  Abydos Temple 159
Adelaide 198
Adirondacks 106
Agen 42
Alakanuk 133
Alaungdaw Kathapa National Park 175
Albany 106
Albury 199, 201
Alexandria 159
Alter do Chão 136, 138
Amarapura 170
  Bagaya Monastery 170
  U-Bein Bridge 170
Amarna 159
Amelia Island 125
Amsterdam 60, 66
  Anne Frank's House 60
  Portuguese Synagogue 61
  Rijksmuseum 12
  Van Gogh Museum 60
Anavilhanas National Park 140
Andalucía 45
Andaman Sea 168
Angsi Glacier 172
Antwerp 11, 13
  Diamond Museum 13
  Grote Markt 11, 13
Apeldoorn 13
Arakan Mountains 171
Aranda de Duero 34
Ardèche 75
Arkansas 119
Arles 74, 76
Arnhem 13
Arribes del Duero Natural Park 34
Aschaffenburg 50
  Schloss Johannisburg 50
Assam Valley 172
Astoria 105
  Astoria Column 105
  Astoria–Megler Bridge 105
  Fort Clatsop National Memorial 105
Astrakhan 94, 98
Aswan 156, 157
  Aswan Botanical Gardens 157
  Aswan Museum 157
  Elephantine Island 157
  Nubian Museum 157
  Sharia al-Souq market 157
Aswan High Dam 156
Athlone 86, 87
Atures Rapids 144, 145
Australian Alps 198
Avignon 74, 75
  Palais des Papes 75
  Pont d'Avignon 75
Ayeyarwady Delta 168, 171
Bacharach 63, 65
Bad Schandau 38
Bagan 171
  Tan-Chi-Taung Mountain 171
Baharampur 178
Baie-Comeau 129
Baltic Sea 36, 95
Bamako 152
Bamberg 48, 49
Banagher 87
Banrock Station winery 199
Barmah National Park 201
Barrancas 144
Basel 66, 70
  Basel Minster 70
  Kunstmuseum Basel 71
  Rathaus 70
  Tinguely Fountain 71
Bassein 171
Batoka Gorge 162
Baton Rouge 115, 117
  Howard Wilkinson Bridge 117–18
  Huey P Long Bridge 118
  Old State Capitol 118
Baton Rouge Bayou 118
Ba Vi National Park 189
Bay of Bengal 172, 176
Bayou Goula Towhead 117
Beardstown 111
Bear Mountain State Park 108
Beaucaire 76
Beaujeu 76–7
Beaune 76
Beijing 195
Belém 136, 139
  Teatro da Paz 139
  Ver-o-Peso 139
Belgrade 23, 79
  Church of St Sava 23
  Kalemegdan fortress 23
  Museum of Yugoslavia 23
Belleville 76
Ben Nevis 15
Bergerac 40
Bernkastel-Kues 55, 56
Bhagalpur 179
Bhamo 170
Black Forest 16, 66, 70
Black Sea 16, 17, 29, 92
Blanc-Sablon 129
Blaye 41
Boca da Valeria 138
Bonneville Dam 104–5
Boppard 63
Bor 26
Bordeaux 40, 42
  Pont de Pierre 42
  Pont Jacques Chaban-Delmas 42
Bourg 41
Braila 27
Bratislava 16, 21
Brazo del Este Natural Park 45
Brazzaville 150
Breakneck Ridge 108
Breisach 66, 70
Bremm 56
Bridge to Nowhere 202, 203
Brig 72
Bruges 11
Bucharest 16, 22, 26–27
  Parliament Palace 23, 26
  Peasant Museum 27
  Revolution Square 23
Buda 16, 92
Budapest 16, 27, 93
  Castle Palace 22
  Chain Bridge 21
  Fisherman's Bastion 22
  Gelert Baths 22
  Parliament 21
  Szechenyi Spa Baths 22
Bumba 151
Burundi 155
Cadillac 42
Cádiz 45, 47
Cahora Bassa 165
Cairo 159
  Blue Mosque 159
  Egyptian Museum 159
  Grand Egyptian Museum 159
  Museum of Islamic Ceramics 159
  Sphinx of Giza 159
Camargue 74, 76
Canal, Beauharnois 127
  Caledonian 14–15
  Chicago Sanitary and Ship 112
  de Garonne 42
  des Deux Mers 42
  du Midi 42
  Elbe-Lübeck 36
  Entre Champagne et Bourgogne 53
  Erie 126
  Grand 87
  Illinois Waterway 110
  Kiel 36, 39
  Latéral de la Marne 52
  Main-Danube 18
  Mariinsk 96
  Moscow 94–5
  Rhine 11
  Rhine-Main-Danube 49
  Royal 87
  Saint-Martin 53
  Suez 159
  Twante 170
Cape Girardeau 121
Carmacks 132
Carpathian Mountains 25
Carrick-on-Shannon 86
Caspian Sea 94, 95, 98
Castets-en-Dorthe 42
Catskill 106
  Catskill Mountains 106
  Clermont State Historic Site 106
Caudebec-en-Caux 84
Cetate 26
Châlons-en-Champagne 52, 53
Chalon-sur-Saône 74, 76
Châteauneuf-du-Pape 75
Château Gaillard 83
Château-Thierry 52
Chautauqua National Wildlife Refuge 111–12
Cherepovets 96
Chester 123
  Elzie C. Segar Memorial Park 123
  Popeye museum 123
Chicago 110, 112
Chickasaw National Wildlife Refuge 120–1
Chioggia 58
Chobe National Park 148
Chongqing 191–2
Chornohora mountains 92
Circle 133
Ciudad Bolivar 144
Ciudad Guayana 144
Clarkston 102
Cliff Cave County Park 123
Côa Museum 34
Côa Valley Archaeological Park 34
Cochem 55, 56
  Reichsburg Castle 55
Cologne 61, 66
  Cathedral 61
  Deutzer Bridge 61
  Gross St Martin Church 61
  Museum Ludwig 62
Columbia Gorge 102
Córdoba 45, 47
  Roman bridge 47
Cordouan Lighthouse 41
Coria del Río 45
Cornwall (USA) 126
Cottian Alps 58
Csongrád 93
Cuerda del Pozo reservoir 34
Cuxhaven 36
Dagana 161
Dales 102, 104
Danube Delta Biosphere Reserve 27
Dawson City 132
Děčín 38
Dendera 156, 158
  Temple of Hathor 158–9
Des Boucles de la Seine Normande nature park 84
Deutsches Eck 56
  Ehrenbreitstein Fortress 56
Diama Dam 160
Dijon 80
Dizy 52
Djerdap Gorge 25
Djerdap National Park 25
Djoudj National Bird Sanctuary 160
Dnipro 29
Donaldsonville 117
Doñana National Park 46
Dordrecht 13
Douro International Natural Park 34
Drayton Island 125
Dresden 38
Dublin 87
Dubna 95
Duong Lam 189
Dürnstein 20
Duruelo de la Sierra 34
Eagle 132
Echuca 201
Edam 13
Edfu temple 158
Eifel 54, 55
Ellis Island 109
El Puerto de Santa María 47
El Toro 145
Emmonak 133
Enniskillen 86
Entre-os-Rios 32
Epernay 52
Esna 158
  Temple of Khnum 158
Fengdu 192
  Fengdu Ghost City 192
  Ming Mountain 192
Five Finger Rapids 132
Florida Everglades 124
Fort William 15
Forty Mile 132
Fort Yukon 133
Frankfurt 48, 50
Ganges Delta 172, 176
Gao 153
George Washington Bridge 109
Ghent 11
Giurgiu 22, 26
Giverny 82
Glasson 87
Glencoe 15
Golden Triangle Park 183
Golubacki Grad 19
Gomantong Caves 181
Goolwa 199
Goring 89
Gotthard Massif 66
Grampian Mountains 15
Grand Île 127
Great Glen 15
Great Lakes 110, 126
Great War Island 78
Green Cove Springs 125
Greenwhich 90
  Cutty Sark 90
Grenoble 74
Guajará Bay 139
Guiana Highlands 142
Gulf of Mexico 110, 114
Gulf of Paría 144
Gulf of St Lawrence 126
Gulf of Tonkin 188
Guwahati 172
  Kamakhya Temple 172
Halong Bay 188
Hamburg 36, 39
  Old Elbe Tunnel 39
  St Michael's Church 39
Ham House 89
Hampton Court Bridge 89
Hampton Court Palace 88, 89
Hanoi 188, 189
  Long Bien Bridge 189
Hautvillers 52
Haverstraw Bay 108–9
Heidelberg 67
Helena 119
Henley 88
Hipango Park 202
Ho Chi Minh City 184, 185
Homalin 174
Hood River 104
Honfleur 80, 85
Huanggang 195
Hudson fjord 106
Hudson Highlands 108
Humber Bridge 109

Hume Dam 201
Hunsrück 54, 55
Hyde Park (USA) 108
    Franklin D. Roosevelt National
      Historic Site 108
Idaho 102
Ijsselmeer 61
Ijsselmeer Sea 13
Île d'Anticosti 129
Île d'Orléans 127
Ilha Pambane 165
Illinois 110
Innsbruck 18
Inverness 15
Iquitos 140, 141
Ivankovo Reservoir 95
Jacksonville 124
Jasenovac 79
Jinghong 182, 183
    Sipsongpanna suspension bridge
      183
Jingzhou 193
Jiuijang 195
    Mount Lushan National Park 195
John Day Dam 102
John James Audubon Bridge 118
Kabara 152
Kalemegdanska Terrace 78
Kalewa 175
Kalna 177
    Rajbari temple complex 177–8
Kalocsa 17
Kampong Cham 187
Kampong Trolach 185
Kasika Conservancy 148
Kazan 98
Kaziranga National Park 173
Kelheim 24, 49
Kemendok National Park 199
Kemendok Nature Reserve 199
Kenner Flur 54
Kherson 29
    St Catherine's Cathedral 29
Khone Falls 182
Khortytsia Island 29
Kichkas Bridge 29
Kiev 29
    St Andrew's Church 29
Killaloe 87
Kinderdijk 12
Kinatangan Wildlife Sanctuary
    181
Kingston (USA) 108
    Hudson River Maritime Museum
      108
    Rondout Creek 108
Kingston upon Thames 88
Kinshasa 150
Kisangani 150, 151
    Cathédrale Notre-Dame du
      Rosaire 151
Kizhi 96
    Preobrazhenskaya Church 96–7
Klondike Gold Rush International
    Historical Park 130
Koblenz 55, 56, 62
    Balduinbrücke 62
    Ehrenbreitstein Castle 62
    Stolzenfels Castle 62
Koh Pen Island 187
Kolkata 173, 176, 177, 178, 179
Kom Ombo 157–8
Koulikoro 153
Kranjska Gora 78
Kratie 184, 187
Kremenchuk 29

Landschaftnyy Park 29
Krems 26
Krkonoše Mountains 36
Kulamba Wildlife Reserve 181
Kulmbach 48
    Plassenburg Castle 48
Lac St-Louis 127
Lac Saint-Pierre 127
Lake, Albert 156
    Alexandrina 198, 199
    Amorim 138
    Atlin 130
    Beloye 96
    Big 111
    Braganca 136, 138
    Curry 111
    Dongting 195
    George 124
    Honghu 195
    Huma 201
    Kariba 162, 164
    Laberge 130, 131
    Lagoda 94, 98
    Leman 72
    Liambezi 148
    Maica 136
    Marai 136
    Meredosia 111
    Michigan 110, 112
    Mulwala 201
    Nasser 156
    Onega 94, 96
    Ontario 126
    Peoria 112
    Rotoaira 202
    Schwatka 131
    Tana 155
    Tear of the Clouds 106
    Tonle Sap 185
    Upper Peoria 112
    Victoria 155
Lake George Conservation Area 125
La Roche-Guyon 82
La Salle 112
Le Havre 80, 85
Le Massif 127
Les Andelys 83
Lesser Three Gorges 193
Liberty Island 109
    Statue of Liberty 109
Libourne 41
Lima 141
Limerick 86
Linz 25, 26
Lisala 150, 151
Lisse 12
Little Alton 110
Little Salmon 132
Livingstone Falls 150
Llovizna Falls 144
Loch Dochfour 15
    Linnhe 15
    Lochy 15
    Ness 15
    Oich 15
London, city area 90
    Canary Wharf 90
    Houses of Parliament 90
    London Eye 90
    Tower of London 90
Lonjsko Polje 79
Lorelei 62–3
    Castle Katz 62
Lorraine 54
Lough Derg 87
Lough Ree 86, 87

Lower Kinabatangan Segama
    Wetlands 181
Lower Lough Erne 86
Lower Zambezi National Park 164
Lower Zambezi Valley 165
Luang Prabang 182–3
Ludwigshafen 67, 69
    Rhein Galerie 69
    Wilhelm-Hack-Museum 69
Luxembourg 54
Luxor 156, 157, 158
    Colossi of Memnon 158
    Karnak Temple 158
    Luxor Temple 158
    Valley of the Kings 158
    Valley of the Queens 158
Lyon 53, 74
Machu Picchu 141
Mâcon 74, 76
    Roche de Solutré 76
Magdeburg 39
Magwe 171
    Myat-thalon Pagoda 171
Maidenhead 89
Mainz 48, 50, 60, 65, 66
    Gutenberg Museum 50, 65
    Mainz Cathedral 65
    Museum of Ancient Seafaring 50
    St Martin's Cathedral 50
    St Stephan Kirche 65
Majuli 172, 173
Makanza 151
Mana Pools National Park 164
Manaus 136, 138, 139–40
    Teatro Amazonas 140
Mandalay 170, 174
    Royal Palace 170
Mandroga 98
Mangapurua Stream 203
Manhattan 109, 126
    Verrazano-Narrows Bridge 109
Manicouagan-Uapishka World
    Biosphere Reserve 129
Mannheim 67, 69
    Kunsthalle Mannheim art muse-
      um 67
Mantes-la-Jolie 82
Mantua 58, 59
Mapledurham 89
Marlow 89
Marseilles 76
Martigny 72
Martigues 76
Massif Central 40
Matiari 178
Mawlaik 175
Maxilly-sur-Saône 53
Mayapur 178
    Temple of the Vedic Planetarium
      178
Mbandaka 150–1
    Equator Stone 151
McNary Dam 102
Meaux 52
    Romanesque cathedral 52
Mediterranean 72, 74, 155, 159
Mein Ma Hla Kyun Wildlife Reserve
    171
Meissen 38
    Albrechtsburg castle 38
Mekong delta 185
Melbourne 198, 201
Melk 26
    Benedictine Abbey 26
Memphis 114, 119, 120
    Mississippi River Museum 120

Mud Island 120
Meredosia National Wildlife
    Refuge 111
Mid-Hudson Bridge 108
Mildura 199
Miles Canyon 130, 131
Miltenberg 49, 50
Mingin 175
Moama 201
Montagne de Reims regional
    park 52
Montélimar 74, 75
Montreal 126
Mont-Sainte-Anne 127
Monywa 174, 175
    Thanboddhay Pagoda 175
Mopti 152
Morrisonville 117
Moscow 94, 98
    Kremlin 94
    Red Square 94
Moselle Ridgeway 55
Mt Hood 104
Mount Marcy 106
Mount Taranaki 202
Mount Tongariro 202
Müden 55
Multnomah Falls 105
Murray Bridge 198
Murshidabad 178
    Hazarduari Palace 178–9
    Katra mosque 179
Myitkyina 170
My Tho 185
    Vĩnh Tràng temple 185
Nam Kan National Park 183
Nanjing 195
    Zhonghua Gate 195
Natchez 119
Natchez National Historical Park 119
Nauta 141
Neptune's Staircase 15
New Madrid 121
New Orleans 114, 115, 116, 117, 120
New York 106
    Empire State Building 106
    World Trade Center 106
Ngaut Ngaut Conservation Park 199
Ngiri Reserve 151
Niger Delta 152
Nile Delta 159
Nizhny Novgorod 98
North Island 202
Novi Sad 17
    Petrovaradin Citadel 17
    Trg Slobode 17
Nuremberg 22, 23, 49
    Cathedral 23
    Toy Museum 23
Oak Alley 116
Oban 15
Ocala National Forest 125
Odenwald mountain 49
Okavango Delta 148–9
Old Scenic Highway 105
    Crown Point 105
Ontario 126
Ópusztaszer National Heritage
    Park 93
Oregon 102, 105
Orinoco Delta 145
Orinokia Bridge 144
Osijek, 17
    Nature Park Kopacki 17

Ostrau 38
Ottawa (USA) 110, 112
Oxford 88
Pacaya Samiria National Reserve
    141
Pak Ou 183
Palatka 125
Palisades 109
Parima Tapirapecó National Park
    144
Paringa 199
    lift bridge 199
Parintins 138
Paris 80
    Eiffel Tower 80
Passau 18
    St Stephen's Cathedral 18
    Veste Oberhaus fortress 20
Patna 179
Pauillac, 41
Pegu Yoma Mountains 171
Pellestrina 58
Peoria 112
    Riverfront Museum 112
Pere Marquette State Park 111
Pest 22, 92
    Chain Bridge 92
    Elisabeth bridge 22
    Liberty bridge 22
Philae 156
    Temple of Isis 156
Phnom Penh 185, 186
    Neak Loeung suspension bridge
      186
    Royal Palace 186
    Tuol Sleng Genocide Museum
      187
Piacenza 59
Pinhão 34
Pipiriki 202
Pirna 38
Plaquemine 117
Plassey 178
    Obelisks of Mir Madan 178
Pocinho 34
Podor 160, 161
Poissy 80
Polesella 58
Pont de Gau Ornithological Park 76
Pont de Normandie suspension
    bridge 85
Portland 105
    Government Island 105
Porto 31–2
    Church of Säo Francisco 31
    Dom Luís I Bridge 32
    Palácio da Bolsa 31
    Ribeira district 31
Port Said 159
Portumna 87
Poughkeepsie 108
Profit bridge 118
Prome 171
Pünderich 55
Putney 90
Quebec City 126, 127
    Citadelle 127
    Fairmont Le Château Frontenac
      127
Queen Elizabeth II bridge 90
Rajmahal 179
Raudales de Guaharibos 144
Red River Delta 188
Regensburg 17
    Porta Praetoria 17
Régua 32

Douro Museum 32
Reims 52
Rheinfelden 71
Rhens 63
Rhine Gorge 62
Rhône Glacier 72
Rice Lake State Fish and Wildlife Area 112
Richard-Toll 161
  Château de Baron Roger 161
Richmond upon Thames 88, 89
Ridgefield National Wildlife Refuge 105
Riesa 38
Rio Grande 144–5
Rio Nanay 140
Rio Negro 138, 140
River, Amazon 136–41
  Arkansas 119
  Atlin 130
  Ayeyarwady 168–71, 174
  Bassein 171
  Blue Nile 155
  Brahmaputra 172–3
  Breg 16
  Brigach 16
  Campaspe 201
  Caroni 144
  Chicago 112
  Chindwin 170, 174–5
  Chobe 148–9
  Columbia 102–5
  Congo 150–1
  Cuando 148
  Curua Una 136
  Da 189
  Daning 193
  Danube 16–27, 29, 49, 78, 79, 92, 93
  Darling 199
  Des Plains 112
  Dhansiri 173
  Dnieper 28–9
  Dogne 40
  Dordogne 40–1, 42
  Dore 40
  Douro 30–5
  Drava 17
  Duong 189
  Durance 74
  East 109
  Elbe 36–9
  Elzbach 55
  Erne 86
  Fortymile 132
  Fox 112
  Ganges 176–9
  Garonne 40, 41, 42–3
  Gironde 40–3
  Grainne 86
  Guadaira 45
  Guadalete 47
  Guadalquivir 44–7
  Hooghly 176, 177, 178, 179
  Huangpu 195
  Hudson 106–9, 126
  Ijssel 61
  Illinois 110–13
  Inn 25
  Isère 74, 75
  Itaya 141
  Ituqui 136
  Jalangi 178
  Kagera 155
  Kinabatangan 180–1
  Kovzha 96

Kupa 79
Les Mayeux 82
Lewis and Clark 105
Linyanti 148
Lower Mekong 184–7
Lualaba 150
Main 48–51
Mali 164
Manicouagan 129
Marañón 141
Marne 52–3
Mincio 59
Mississippi 110, 114–23
Moscow 94
Moselle 50, 54–7, 62
Murray 198–201
Myittha 175
Nam Ou 183
Neckar 50, 67
Nederrijn 61
Neva 98
Niger 152–3
Nile 154–9
Nmai 168
Noord 12
Ohio 121
Orinoco 142–5
Pelly 132
Petit Rhône 76
Ploučnice 38
Po 58–9
Red 188–9
Red Main 48
Rhine 12, 22, 48, 49, 50, 53, 54, 55, 56, 60–71
Rhône 72–7
Ruak 183
Saar 54
St Charles 127
St Johns 124–5
St Lawrence 126–9
Saint-Maurice 127
Sangamon 110
Saône 72–7
Sava 19, 78–9
Scheldt 11
Sheksna 96
Snake 102
Solimoes 138
Song Lo 189
Sông Trà Lý 189
Svir 94–9
Tameqa 32
Tapajós 136
Teslin 130, 131
Thái Bình 188, 189
Thames 88–91, 136
Tonle Sap 185, 187
Ucayali 141
Upper Mekong 182–3
Valeria 138
Volga 94–9
Vytegra 96
Whanganui 202–3
White 132
White Main 48
White Nile 155
Yangon 170, 171
Yangtze 190–5
Yukon 130–3
Zambezi 148, 149, 162–5
Rotterdam 12, 13
  Harbour Museum 13

Rouen 83, 84, 85
  Ile Lacroix 84
  Rouen Cathedral 84
Roumare National Forest 84
Rousse 26
  National Transport Museum 26
Royal Victoria Docks 90
Royan 41
Rüdesheim 63
  Bromersburg Wine Museum 63
  Siegreid's Mechanical Music Museum 63
Runnymede 89
Rybinsk reservoir 95
Sagaing 170
Saguenay 129
Saint-Aubin-sur-Quilleboeuf 85
St Augustine 125
St Augustus 15
  Castle Urquhart 15
Sainte-Foy-la-Grande 41
Saint-Émilion 41
Saintes-Maries-de-la-Mer 76
St Lawrence Seaway 126
Saint-Louis (Senegal) 160
  Faidherbe Bridge 160
  Langue de Barbarie spit 160
St Louis (USA) 110, 123
  Centennial Park 123
  Gateway Arch 123
  Laclede's Landing 123
St Paul 115
St Petersburg 94, 98
  Catherine Palace 98
  Hermitage Museum 98
  St Petersburg Ballet 98
Saint-Pierre-de-Boeuf 75
  Île de la Platiàre nature reserve 75
Saint-Pierre-d'Eyraud 40
Salamanca 34
Samara 98
Samara Oblast dam 98
Sandakan 180, 181
  Puu Jih Shih Temple 181
Sanlúcar de Barrameda 47
Santarém 136, 138
São João da Pesqueira 34
Saratov 98
Sauternes 42
Saxon Switzerland National Park 38
Schweinfurt 49
Segou 152
Sept-Iles 129
Seville 45
  Torre del Oro 45
  Triana Bridge 45
Shanghai 191, 195
Shannonbridge 86
Shannon-Erne Waterway 86
Shannon Estuary 86
Shibaozhai 192
Shillong plateau 172
Shishou 195
Shreve's Bar 118–19
Siem Reap 185
  Angkor 185
Silghat 173
Silistra 21
Singu Plateau 170
Sip 26
Sisak 78, 79
Sitthaung 175
Sleepy Hollow 108
Smolensk 29
Soria 34

Source-Seine 80
Southend 90
Spanish Pyrenees 42
Speyer 69
  Cathedral of St Mary and St Stephen 69
  medieval synagogue 69
Springfield 110–11
  Abraham Lincoln Presidential Library and Museum 111
Staines 88
Starved Rock State Park 112
Steigerwald Lake National Wildlife Refuge 105
Stevenson 104
Storm King 108
Strasbourg 53, 66, 69
  Archaeological Museum 70
  Grande Ile 69–70
  Notre-Dame Cathedral 70
  Palais des Rohan 70
Sukau 181
Sulu Sea 180
Sunshine Bridge 116–17
Swiss Alps 60, 72
Szeged 93
  Szeged Synagogue 93
  Votive Church 93
Taglio Di Pô 58
Tamanthi Wildlife Reserve 174
Tân Châu 186
  Standalone Sam Mountain 186
Tappan Zee 109
Tarascon 76
Tarouca 32
  Monastery of Saint John of Tarouca 32
  Ucanha bridge 32
Tasman Sea 202
Taumarunui 202
Teddington Lock 88, 89
Thái Bình 189
Thayetmyo 171
Thirty Miles (Yukon) 131
  Shipyard Island 131
Thousand Islands 126
  Wolfe Island 126
Three Gorges 191, 192
Three Gorges Dam 191, 193
Tibetan Plateau 182, 191
Tilbury 90, 136
Timbuktu 152
Timucuan Ecological and Historic Preserve 124
Tiszafüred 93
Titisee 70
Tokaj 93
Toulouse 42
Toungdoot 174–3
Tournon 75
Traben-Trarbach 55
  Brückentor gatehouse 55
Trier 54, 56
  Porta Nigra gate 54
Troy (USA) 106
Tupinambarana Island 138
Turin 58
  Ponte Isabella 59
Uglich 95, 98
  St Dmitri-on-the-Blood church 95
Upper Lough Erne 86
Vaidai Hills 94
Val d'Isère 74
Valence 74
  Castle Crussol 75

Varosa Valley 32
Vega de Terrón 34
Venetian Delta Regional Park 58
Venice 58
  Bridge of Sighs 58
  Grand Canal 58
  St Mark's Basilica 58
Vernon 82
Veste Oberhaus fortress 20
Vexin Français Natural Regional Park 82
Vicksburg 119
Victoria Falls 162
Vienna 16, 20
  Belvedere Museum 20
  St Stephen's Cathedral 20
  Schönbrunn Palace 21
  Vienna State Opera 20
Vienne 74
Viet Tri 189
Vila Nova de Gaia 31
Villequier 85
Vinhateiro 31, 34
Vĩnh Long 185
Vitry-le-François 52
Volendam 13
Volga delta 98
Volkach 49
Volograd dam 98
Vosges Mountains 54
Vukovar 23
Wachau Valley 26
Wallingford 89
Washington 102
West Point 108
Whanganui 202
Whanganui National Park 202, 203
Whitehorse 130–1
Windsor 89
Windsor Castle 88
Wittenberg 38
  Luther's House 38
  St Marien's Church 38
Worms 66–7
Wuhan 191, 195
  First Yangtze River Bridge 195
Würzburg 48, 49
  Fortress Marienberg 49
  Residenz Palace 49
Xian 195
Xuan Thuy National Park 188
Yangambi Biosphere Reserve 151
Yangon 171
Yarlung Tsangpo 172
Yaroslavl 95, 98
  Spaso-Preobrazhensky monastery 95
Yenangyaung 171
Yichang 191, 192, 193
Yueyang 195
Yukon-Charley Rivers National Preserve 133
Yukon Delta National Wildlife Refuge 133
Yukon Flats National Wildlife Reserve 133
Yunnan 188
Zaanse Schans 12
Zambezi Delta 165
Zamora 34
  Cathedral 34
Zaporizhia 29
Zelenci nature reserve 78
Zhiguli Mountains 98

First published in the United Kingdom in 2018 by John Beaufoy Publishing,
11 Blenheim Court, 316 Woodstock Road, Oxford OX2 7NS, England
www.johnbeaufoy.com

10 9 8 7 6 5 4 3 2 1

ISBN 978-1-912081-94-3

Designed by Ginny Zeal
Cartography by William Smuts
Project management by Rosemary Wilkinson

Printed and bound in Malaysia by Times Offset (M) Sdn. Bhd.